CCNP Cisco Networking Academy Program: Multilayer Switching Lab Companion

Cisco Systems, Inc.
Cisco Networking Academy Program
Wayne Lewis, Ph.D.

Cisco Press

201 West 103rd Street
Indianapolis, IN 46290 USA

CCNP Cisco Networking Academy Program: Multilayer Switching Lab Companion

Cisco Systems, Inc.
Cisco Networking Academy Program
Wayne Lewis, Ph.D.

Published by:
Cisco Press
210 West 103rd Street
Indianapolis, IN 46290 USA

Printed in the United States of America   1 2 3 4 5 6 7 8 9 0

First Printing   November 2002

ISBN: 1-58713-034-3

Warning and Disclaimer

This book is designed to provide information on multilayer switching. Every effort has been made to make this book as complete and accurate as possible, but no warranty or fitness is implied.

The information is provided on an "as is" basis. The author, Cisco Press, and Cisco Systems, Inc. shall have neither liability nor responsibility to any person or entity with respect to any loss or damages arising from the information contained in this book or from the use of the programs that may accompany it.

The opinions expressed in this book belong to the author and are not necessarily those of Cisco Systems, Inc.

Trademark Acknowledgments

All terms mentioned in this book that are known to be trademarks or service marks have been appropriately capitalized. Cisco Press or Cisco Systems, Inc., cannot attest to the accuracy of this information. Use of a term in this book should not be regarded as affecting the validity of any trademark or service mark.

Feedback Information

At Cisco Press, our goal is to create in-depth technical books of the highest quality and value. Each book is crafted with care and precision, undergoing rigorous development that involves the unique expertise of members of the professional technical community.

Reader feedback is a natural continuation of this process. If you have any comments regarding how we could improve the quality of this book, or otherwise alter it to better suit your needs, you can contact us at networkingacademy@ciscopress.com. Please be sure to include the book title and ISBN in your message.

We greatly appreciate your assistance.

Publisher	John Wait
Editor-in-Chief	John Kane
Executive Editor	Carl Lindholm
Cisco Representative	Anthony Wolfenden
Cisco Press Program Manager	Sonia Torress Chavez
Cisco Marketing Communications Manager	Tom Geitner
Cisco Marketing Program Manager	Edie Quiroz
Production Manager	Patrick Kanouse
Development Editor	Ginny Bess Munroe
Senior Editor	Sheri Cain
Project Editor	San Dee Phillips
Technical Editors	Barb Nolley
	Stanford Wong
	Todd White
	Howard Rahmlow
Copy Editor	Gayle Johnson

CISCO SYSTEMS

Corporate Headquarters
Cisco Systems, Inc.
170 West Tasman Drive
San Jose, CA 95134-1706
USA
http://www.cisco.com
Tel: 408 526-4000
    800 553-NETS (6387)
Fax: 408 526-4100

European Headquarters
Cisco Systems Europe
11 Rue Camille Desmoulins
92782 Issy-les-Moulineaux
Cedex 9
France
http://www-europe.cisco.com
Tel: 33 1 58 04 60 00
Fax: 33 1 58 04 61 00

Americas Headquarters
Cisco Systems, Inc.
170 West Tasman Drive
San Jose, CA 95134-1706
USA
http://www.cisco.com
Tel: 408 526-7660
Fax: 408 527-0883

Asia Pacific Headquarters
Cisco Systems Australia,
Pty., Ltd
Level 17, 99 Walker Street
North Sydney
NSW 2059 Australia
http://www.cisco.com
Tel: +61 2 8448 7100
Fax: +61 2 9957 4350

Cisco Systems has more than 200 offices in the following countries. Addresses, phone numbers, and fax numbers are listed on the Cisco Web site at www.cisco.com/go/offices

Argentina • Australia • Austria • Belgium • Brazil • Bulgaria • Canada • Chile • China • Colombia • Costa Rica • Croatia • Czech Republic • Denmark • Dubai, UAE • Finland • France • Germany • Greece • Hong Kong • Hungary • India • Indonesia • Ireland Israel • Italy • Japan • Korea • Luxembourg • Malaysia • Mexico • The Netherlands • New Zealand • Norway • Peru • Philippines Poland • Portugal • Puerto Rico • Romania • Russia • Saudi Arabia • Scotland • Singapore • Slovakia • Slovenia • South Africa • Spain Sweden • Switzerland • Taiwan • Thailand • Turkey • Ukraine • United Kingdom • United States • Venezuela • Vietnam • Zimbabwe

About the Author

Wayne Lewis is the Cisco academy manager for the Pacific Center for Advanced Technology Training, based at Honolulu Community College (HCC). Since 1998, Wayne has taught Networking Academy instructors from universities, colleges, and high schools in Australia, Canada, Central America, China, Hong Kong, Indonesia, Mexico, Romania, Russia, Singapore, South America, Taiwan, and the U.S., both onsite and at HCC. Prior to teaching computer networking, Wayne began teaching math at age 20 at Wichita State University, followed by the University of Hawaii and HCC. Wayne received a Ph.D. in math from the University of Hawaii in 1992. Wayne works as a contractor for Cisco Systems Worldwide Education, developing curriculum for the Networking Academy Program. Wayne enjoys surfing the North Shore of Oahu when he's not distracted by work.

Acknowledgments

Mom, thanks for showing me how to realize my goals and keep a positive attitude. Dad, thanks for instilling in me a love of learning and scientific pursuit. Thanks to my brother, Richard, for keeping me out of worse trouble than I managed to find. Thanks to my sisters, Nancy, Barbara, Debra, and Sandra, for showing me the things I want to see come true for my daughters. Okaasan, thanks for always being there for our family in Hawaii.

Ginny Bess Munroe, Carl Lindholm, Tracy Hughes, Sheri Cain, and Patrick Kanouse at Cisco Press, thanks so much for keeping me on track and providing the professional guidance that made this effort possible. Ginny and Tracy have made the deadline and content and format business as enjoyable as is humanly possible.

Thanks to Kevin Johnston and Todd White of Cisco Systems for being the founders of the CCNP Academy Program. This book is built on their efforts. Thanks to George Ward of Cisco Systems for creating the Cisco Networking Academy Program; were it not for his vision, I would not have had the opportunity to start a career in computer networking education. Thanks to Dennis Frezzo of Cisco Systems for his guidance in all things Cisco Academy-related; without Dennis, there would be no voice for the students and instructors in the Networking Academy Program. I am especially thankful to Vito Amato of Cisco Systems for giving me the opportunity to write this book; Vito has been 100 percent supportive of my work since I met him. Alex Belous of Cisco Systems doesn't get the acclaim he deserves because he's always working behind the scenes, making things happen. Thanks, Alex, for providing support when no one is aware of it.

I want to thank my CATC partner, Dallas Shiroma, for showing me what a good teacher is. Dallas serves as the ideal role model for teachers. Year after year, Dallas selflessly and diligently continues to provide the best in science and technology education. Don Bourassa and Ramsey Pedersen are my bosses at Honolulu Community College. I cannot say enough about how grateful I am to them for paving the career path for me that began in 1993. Ramsey has been absolutely supportive of me from the beginning. Don is a great boss who leads in a way that all want to follow.

Mark McGregor blazed the trail for me to follow in writing this book. Thanks, Mark, for setting a standard for curriculum development for which we can all strive.

Special thanks go to this book's technical reviewers: Barb Nolley, Stanford Wong, Todd White, and Howard Rahmlow. They have once again done an incredible job of improving the original draft.

Thanks to the Hawaii CCIE Group Study: Stanford (the godfather), Michael Jordan, Rob Rummel, Frank Buffington, Nick Pandya, Robert Yee, Torrey Suzuki, Edwin Lacaden, and Errol Gorospe.

Finally, I'd like to thank the folks I work with on the CCNP currdev teams. I feel privileged to work with you: Andrew Chan, Jim Yoshida, Brian Sterck, Terry Koziniec, Steve Richards, and Nick Pandya.

Table of Contents

Introduction

CCNP Cisco Networking Academy Program: Multilayer Switching Lab Companion supplements your study of the multilayer switching concepts in the Cisco Networking Academy Program. This book is also useful in its own right as a Cisco multilayer switching lab exercise manual. Through easy-to-follow lab exercises, this book provides intermediate- and advanced-level students with the lab skills necessary to pass the CCNP switching exam (BCMSN) and to further their career opportunities in computer networking.

Concepts covered in this book include campus network design, VLANs, Spanning Tree Protocol (STP), inter-VLAN routing, Hot Standby Router Protocol (HSRP), security with Catalyst switches, and the role of multicasting in campus LANs.

As with all advanced networking topics, you will find that your studies are best complemented by a text that describes the theory and foundational concepts introduced in the hands-on lab exercises. To that end, Cisco Press offers *CCNP Cisco Networking Academy Program: Multilayer Switching Companion Guide*, which includes thorough treatments of the networking topics discussed in this lab manual.

Who Should Read This Book

This book's audience includes students who are seeking advanced Cisco switching configuration skills and certification. In particular, this book is targeted at students in the CCNP Cisco Networking Academy Program, which is offered in schools around the world. In the classroom, this book can serve as a substitute for the labs appearing in the online curriculum.

Another audience for this book includes network engineers presently working in the industry and individuals striving to become network engineers. This book was designed to have a broad appeal and is useful as a lab manual for anyone learning multilayer switching. For corporations and academic institutions to take advantage of the capabilities of modern networking, a large number of individuals need to be trained in the design and operation of networks.

This Book's Organization

This book is broken into chapters corresponding to the chapters in the companion guide. (No labs appear in Chapters 1, 2, and 7 of the curriculum.) This book also includes two appendixes.

Chapter 3, "Switch Administration," introduces you to the command line and the basic management of Catalyst switches.

Chapter 4, "Introduction to VLANs," explains the various types of VLANs. It covers how you decide to best deploy VLANs in a campus network and how you configure VLANs on Catalyst switches.

Chapter 5, "Spanning Tree Protocol," describes in detail the operation of STP in campus networks. It also covers configuring STP and STP design implications.

Chapter 6, "Inter-VLAN Routing," demonstrates the configuration of routing between VLANs using Cisco routers or route processors specific to the various Catalyst switch platforms.

Chapter 8, "Hot Standby Router Protocol," details the use of HSRP to provide Layer 3 redundancy in the context of the core-distribution-access campus network model.

Chapter 9, "Multicasting," provides an exhaustive survey of the multicast protocols used today to enable the propagation of rich multimedia content over campus networks.

Chapter 10, "Security," describes how to create a security policy and secure Catalyst switches in a campus network.

Appendix A, "Command Reference," provides a useful reference for the usage of each command used in Cisco multilayer switching.

Appendix B, "Cisco IOS, CatOS, and CatIOS" explains how the "set-based" operating system, known as CatOS, compares to the operating system that is replacing it, CatIOS (IOS for Catalyst switches).

This Book's Features

This book contains several elements that help you learn about advanced networking and Cisco IOS technologies:

- **Figures and tables**—This book contains figures and tables that help explain concepts, commands, and procedures. Figures illustrate network layouts and processes, and examples provide sample IOS configurations. In addition, tables provide command summaries and comparisons of features and characteristics.
- **Questions**—Numerous questions included in the laboratory exercises are designed to elicit particular points of understanding. These questions help verify your comprehension of the technology being implemented.

The conventions used to present command syntax in this book are the same conventions used in the *Cisco IOS Command Reference*:

- **Bold** indicates commands and keywords that are entered literally as shown. In examples (not syntax), bold indicates user input (for example, a **show** command).
- *Italic* indicates arguments for which you supply values.
- Braces ({ }) indicate a required element.
- Square brackets ([ ]) indicate an optional element.
- Vertical bars (|) separate alternative, mutually exclusive elements.
- Braces and vertical bars within square brackets (such as [x {y | z}]) indicate a required choice within an optional element. You do not need to enter what is in the brackets, but if you do, you have some required choices in the braces.

Lab Equipment Requirements

CCNP Networking Academies

Each lab in this lab companion is written to accommodate the CCNP Academy lab bundles, which CCNP Cisco Networking Academies are required to maintain. The majority of the labs require a Catalyst 4006 switch and a Catalyst 2900 XL switch. (A Catalyst 2900 XL can be substituted with a Catalyst 2950, 3500 XL, or 3550 switch.) Many labs also require Cisco 2620 and/or Cisco 2621 routers in addition to the 4006 and 2900 XL switches. The Catalyst 4006 switch is assumed to have a Supervisor Engine II in slot 1 and the Layer 3 Services Module in slot 2. With the Economy bundle, you can create one "pod" with the equipment required for the labs. With the Standard bundle, you can create two pods with the equipment required for the labs.

Some Academies prefer to mount each pod in a fixed rack for remote access in the Cisco lab. Other Academies prefer to use the distributed approach, in which equipment is moved to convenient locations during each lab session, either by carrying the equipment or by using a mobile pod. There is no "best" way for students to access equipment at your site. It depends on the variables in play at your site. The fixed-pod approach has the advantage of allowing remote access and not requiring you to recable the equipment for each lab. This approach assumes that the set of labs is designed to allow this (so that recabling is not required). Lab designers often prefer flexibility in topologies to effectively teach various concepts. The distributed approach has the advantage of flexibility and mobility, should you have multiple Cisco lab locations or should you frequently make topological changes that preclude a fixed-pod approach.

Chapter 9 labs require IP/TV software (the demo version, which is available at www.cisco.com/warp/public/cc/pd/mxsv/iptv3400, is adequate). Some Academies have proactively pursued other options for testing multicast functionality. Be aware that some products marketed as multicasting products actually perform UDP streaming (not true multicast), so be sure that you're getting the real thing.

Chapter 10 labs require CiscoSecure Access Control Server software (which you get with your CCNP bundle). Versions 2.4 and 2.6 have been tested with the labs. You can download the Semester 6 CiscoSecure ACS Configuration File and modify the usernames, passwords, and TACACS+ keys for use in Chapter 10 labs.

Workstations with terminal emulation programs, Ethernet NICs, TCP/IP software, and a web browser are required for the labs in this course. All the labs were written and tested using Microsoft Windows 98, 2000, and XP machines.

Independent Lab Environments

If you do not have access to a CCNP Academy lab bundle, you can build your own pod with the appropriate Cisco routers and switches. For these labs, we recommend a Catalyst 4006 with a Supervisor Engine II and a Layer 3 Services module, a Catalyst 2900 XL or 2950 switch, two Cisco 2621 routers (each with a WIC-2A/S), and one Cisco 2620 router (with a WIC-2A/S). In addition, you need DTE/DCE cables to connect the synchronous serial interfaces.

Other Considerations

These lab exercises were written and tested primarily using Cisco IOS Release 12.0(5)T. Although this release is not required to run these labs, note that some features and command syntax change with each Cisco IOS release. CatOS Release 7.3 was used on the Catalyst 4006 Supervisor Engine II.

A diagram containing the essential configuration information precedes each exercise. Because the labs can be performed on a variety of equipment, the interface numbering in the lab diagrams might not match your specific devices. Command output, when included in the labs, reflects what you see if you use the standard CCNP Academy lab bundle.

Lab 3-1: Upgrading the 4006 Supervisor Software

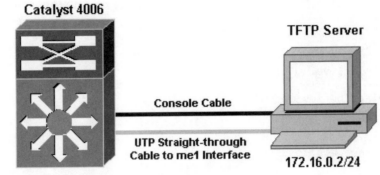

Objective

It is possible that when the new Catalyst 4006 arrives with the Supervisor Engine II and the Layer 3 Services module, the Supervisor module will not recognize the L3 module. The software image on the Supervisor module must be at least Catalyst OS 5.5(4) to recognize the L3 module. Many early shipments came with CatOS 5.4(2) or older. This set of instructions demonstrates how to upgrade the software image.

This process works for any CatOS upgrade of the Supervisor Engine II.

Scenario

A WS-X4232-L3 Layer 3 Services module has been added to an existing 4006 chassis. After installing it, you discover that the Supervisor module does not recognize the new L3 module. A check of the configuration shows that the Supervisor CatOS image is too old to support the new L3 module. The following steps describe the process of upgrading the software.

Step 1

To confirm the software version, use the **show config** command while connected to the Supervisor module via the console port (rollover cable). *Note*: If you haven't used the Catalyst 4006 before, you move to privileged (enable) mode the same way as on other Cisco devices (type **enable**). If you haven't set passwords on the switch, just press **Enter** each time you are prompted for a password:

```
Console> (enable)
Console> (enable) show config
This command shows non-default configurations only.
Use 'show config all' to show both default and non-default configurations.
..........
..................
..

begin
!
# ***** NON-DEFAULT CONFIGURATION *****
!
```

```
#time: Wed Apr 18 2001, 14:46:47
!
#version 5.4(2)                          (Shows the current version)
!
#system web interface version(s)
!
#test
set test diaglevel minimal
!
#frame distribution method
set port channel all distribution mac both
!
#ip
set interface sl0 down
!
#syslog
set logging level cops 2 default
!
#set boot command
set boot config-register 0x2
set boot system flash bootflash:cat4000.5-4-2.bin
  (Shows image used)
!
#mls
set mls nde disable
!
#port channel
set port channel 1/1-2 1
!
#module 1 : 2-port 1000BaseX Supervisor
!
#module 2 empty
!
#module 3 empty
!
#module 4 empty
!
#module 5 empty
!
#module 6 empty
end
```

The L3 module is module 2 (slot 2 from the top) on your unit. The "empty" instances in the output confirm that the Supervisor module does not recognize the new L3 module.

Step 2 (Optional for Students)

The following steps describe the process of downloading the image from the www.cisco.com site. *Students*: The instructor will tell you where to find the appropriate image.

Go to www.cisco.com (the Cisco.com web site) and log in with your account information based on your SMARTnet agreement. Choose **Software Center** from the Service & Support section, as shown in the following figure.

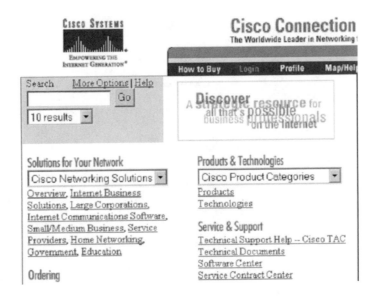

Choose **LAN Switching Software** from the Software Products & Downloads list, as shown here.

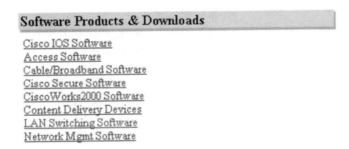

Choose Catalyst 4000 from the list of Catalyst Switch Software choices.

● Catalyst Switch Software

Catalyst 1200	Catalyst 3500XL
Catalyst 1600	Catalyst 3900
Catalyst 1700	Catalyst 4000
Catalyst 1800	Catalyst 4232

Choose the version by clicking the link. The newest version is near the bottom.

Select a File to Download

Filename	Description	Release	Size 'Bytes'	More Info
cat4000-cv.5-4-1.bin	Catalyst 4000 Ciscoview ADP Flash Code	5.4(1)	2197413	?
cat4000-cv.5-5-1.bin	Catalyst 4000 Ciscoview ADP Flash Code	5.5(1)	2239867	?
cat4000-cv.5-5-2.bin	Catalyst 4000 Ciscoview ADP Flash Code	5.5(2)	2223426	?
cat4000-cv.5-5-3.bin	Catalyst 4000 Ciscoview ADP Flash Code	5.5(3)	2223426	?
cat4000-cv.5-5-5.bin	Catalyst 4000 Ciscoview ADP Flash Code	5.5(5)	2223426	?
cat4000-cv.6-1-1.bin	Catalyst 4000 Ciscoview ADP Flash Code	6.1(1)	2512556	?
cat4000-promupgrade.5-5-4.bin	Cat4000 Rommon Upgrade	5.5(4)	1895680	?
cat4000-releasenote.4-5-11.pdf	Catalyst 4000 Release Notes	4.5(11)	154716	?
cat4000-releasenote.5-5-6.pdf	Catalyst 4000 Release Notes	5.5(6)	221644	?
cat4000-releasenote.5-5-7.pdf	Catalyst 4000 Release Notes	5.5(7)	1514344	?
cat4000-releasenote.6-1-2.pdf	Catalyst 4000 Release Notes	6.1(2)	345772	?
cat4000-releasenote.6-1-3.pdf	Catalyst 4000 Release Notes	6.1(3)	432886	?
cat4000-releasenote.6-2-1.pdf	Catalyst 4000 Release Notes	6.2(1)	388452	?
cat4000.4-5-10.bin	Catalyst 4000 Image	4.5(10)	2843352	?
cat4000.4-5-11.bin	Catalyst 4000 Image	4.5(11)	2846020	?
cat4000.5-5-4b.bin	Catalyst 4000 Image	5.5(4b)	3642740	?
cat4000.5-5-5.bin	Catalyst 4000 Image	5.5(5)	3643984	?
cat4000.5-5-6.bin	Catalyst 4000 Image	5.5(6)	3646588	?
cat4000.5-5-7.bin	Catalyst 4000 Image	5.5(7)	3648964	?
cat4000.6-1-1.bin	Catalyst 4000 Image	6.1(1)	3817476	?
cat4000.6-1-2.bin	Catalyst 4000 Image	6.1(2)	3830900	?
cat4000.6-1-3.bin	Catalyst 4000 Image	6.1(3)	3834504	?
cat4000.6-2-1.bin	Catalyst 4000 Image	6.2(1)	4089736	?

Agree to the Software License Agreement when you are prompted. Pick a Download Site and then just follow the normal download instructions.

Step 3

The upgrade process uses TFTP very much like the CCNA and other CCNP exercises, with just a couple twists unique to this model of switch.

Make sure that the TFTP server is running and that the software image is in the server's default directory. Note the IP address of the TFTP server.

Cabling—Use a straight-through RJ-45 UTP patch cord to connect the Supervisor module out-of-band management port (10/100 me1 interface) to the TFTP server's NIC. If you go through a switch to get to the TFTP server, you need to use a crossover cable between the 4006 and the switch. The pinout for the me1 interface is the same as that of a standard switch port.

Note: The 10/100 out-of-band me1 interface is the port on the Supervisor module labeled "10/100 MGT." It is not a normal switch port, but rather an Ethernet interface that can be used to administer the switch from an independent management network (thus the term *out-of-band* management). This port can be connected to an independent Ethernet network that is not part of your normal production network. If the production network fails for some reason, out-of-band management allows you to still communicate with the switch through this external Ethernet interface. The me1 interface acts much like a NIC card on a workstation.

Configuring the me1 interface—The me1 interface must be assigned an address in the same subnet as the TFTP server. Here are the commands to set the me1 from the enable prompt:

```
Console> (enable) set interface me1 172.16.0.5 255.255.255.0
Interface me1 IP address and netmask set.
Console> (enable)
```

Verify the change by using the **show config** command:

```
Console> (enable) show config
This command shows non-default configurations only.
begin
!
# ***** NON-DEFAULT CONFIGURATION *****
!
#time: Wed Apr 18 2001, 14:48:43
!
#version 5.4(2)
!
#system web interface version(s)
!
#test
set test diaglevel minimal
!
#frame distribution method
set port channel all distribution mac both
!
#ip
set interface sl0 down
set interface me1 172.16.0.5 255.255.255.0 172.16.0.255   (here it is)
!
#syslog
set logging level cops 2 default
!
<output omitted>
```

Step 4

Confirm connectivity with the TFTP server by pinging it:

```
Console> (enable) ping 172.16.0.2
!!!!!

----172.16.0.2 PING Statistics----
5 packets transmitted, 5 packets received, 0% packet loss
round-trip (ms)  min/avg/max = 14/15/17
Console> (enable)
```

Note: On some versions of the Cisco IOS Software, you get a "172.16.0.2 is alive" message instead of the typical Cisco ping output.

If this fails, check that the TFTP server is on, check the IP addresses, and check that the cabling is correct (see Step 3). Troubleshoot as needed.

Step 5

Use the **show flash** command to check the contents of Flash to confirm that space is available for the new image. It will ultimately reside there with the existing image(s):

```
Console> (enable) show flash
-#- ED --type-- --crc--- -seek-- nlen -length- -----date/time------ name
  1 .. ffffffff 548c8f9c  39cf70   17  3526384 --- -- ---- --:--:-- cat4000.5-4-2.bin

12071928 bytes available (3526384 bytes used)
Console> (enable)
```

Step 6

To make sure that you have a backup of the current image, first copy the current image to the TFTP server. In addition to creating a backup, this step familiarizes you with the steps and the time required before you start copying the new image into the 4006.

You must enter the TFTP server IP address and the current image name. This final item is case-sensitive, so it might be best to copy it from the **show flash** output and paste it:

```
Console> (enable) copy flash tftp
Flash device [bootflash]?
Name of file to copy from []? cat4000.5-4-2.bin
IP address or name of remote host []? 172.16.0.2
Name of file to copy to []? cat4000.5-4-2.bin (You could rename here)
CCCCCCCCCCCCCCCCCCCCCCCCCCCCCCCCCCCCCCCCCCCCCCCCCCCCCCCCCCCCCCCCCCCCCCCC
CCCCCCCCCCCCCCCCCCCCCCCCCCCCCCCCCCCCCCCCCCCCCCCCCCCCCCCX
File has been copied successfully.

Console> (enable)
```

The **X** shown at the end of the second row of Cs represents a character wide spinning-line segment that looks very much like a turnstile. It appears on the screen for several minutes until the copy operation is done. It is a 4 MB file, so it takes several minutes to copy.

Step 7

You are ready to download the image to Flash. **Suggestion:** Use Microsoft Windows Explorer on the TFTP server, select the new image name to highlight the text of the filename (as if you were going to rename it), and do a copy. You will paste this when the **copy tftp** command asks for the filename.

Note that the following default values for each prompt assume that you did the **copy flash tftp** step earlier. Because of the earlier steps, you can just press **Enter** at the first prompt. Press **Enter** at prompts 3 and 4 unless you want to rename the image:

```
Console> (enable) copy tftp flash
IP address or name of remote host [172.16.0.2]?
Name of file to copy from [cat4000. 5-4-2.bin]? cat4000.6-2-1.bin
Flash device [bootflash]?
Name of file to copy to [cat4000.6-2-1.bin]?
7981064 bytes available on device bootflash, proceed (y/n) [n]? y
XCCCCCCCCCCCCCCCCCCCCCCCCCCCCCCCCCCCCCCCCCCCCCCCCCCCCCCCCCCCCCCCCCC
CCCCCCCCCCCCCCCCCCCCCCCCCCCCCCCCCCCCCCCCCCCCCCCCCCCCCCCCCCCCC
File has been copied successfully.

Console> (enable)
```

The **X** shown before the first row of Cs represents a spinning-line segment that looks like a turnstile. It appears on the screen for several minutes until the copy is done. This is exactly the opposite of when you copy to the TFTP server.

Step 8

To confirm that the image download worked, use the **show flash** command. You see that both images are now present:

```
Console> (enable) show flash
-#- ED --type-- --crc--- -seek-- nlen -length- -----date/time------ name
  1 .. ffffffff 548c8f9c  39cf70   17  3526384 --- -- ---- --:--:-- cat4000.5-4-2.bin
  2 .. ffffffff d39d5c46  783778   17  4089736 Apr 17 2001 14:40:15 cat4000.6-2-1.bin

7981192 bytes available (7616376 bytes used)

Console> (enable)
```

Step 9

Use the **set boot system flash bootflash:** *image_name* **prepend** command to tell the 4006 which image to use. It is critical that you add the prepend option to the end of this command to move this image ahead of the existing image. They will both be listed on the configuration. If you forget this option, the machine will boot to the old image.

The first set of output that follows uses the help feature to view the options:

```
Console> (enable) set boot system flash bootflash:cat4000.6-2-1.bin ?
  prepend                Put as first priority
  <mod>                  Module number
  <cr>
Console> (enable) set boot system flash bootflash:cat4000.6-2-1.bin prepend

Console> (enable)
```

Use the **show config** command to confirm that the command worked. The following includes only the relevant output:

```
Console> (enable) show config
!
```

```
#set boot command
set boot config-register 0x2
set boot system flash bootflash:cat4000.6-2-1.bin
set boot system flash bootflash:cat4000.5-4-2.bin
!
```

Step 10

Reboot the device with the **reset** command. The configuration is automatically saved on a 4006 so that you do not need to do a **copy run start** command as you would on a Cisco router.

Use the **show config** and **show module** commands to confirm that the changes have been made:

```
Console> (enable) show config
This command shows non-default configurations only.
Use 'show config all' to show both default and non-default configurations.
..........
..................
..

begin
!
# ***** NON-DEFAULT CONFIGURATION *****
!
#time: Wed Apr 18 2001, 15:04:09
!
#version 6.2(1)                        (Note the new version)
!
#system web interface version(s)
!
#test
set test diaglevel minimal
!
#frame distribution method
set port channel all distribution mac both
!
#ip
set interface sl0 down
set interface me1 172.16.0.5 255.255.255.0 172.16.0.255
!
#syslog
set logging level cops 2 default
!
#set boot command
set boot config-register 0x2
set boot system flash bootflash:cat4000.6-2-1.bin
set boot system flash bootflash:cat4000.5-4-2.bin   (This is ignored. Can be
removed)
!
#mls
set mls nde disable
!
#port channel
set port channel 1/1-2 1
!
#module 1 : 2-port 1000BaseX Supervisor
!
#module 2 empty
```

```
!
#module 3 : 34-port Router Switch Card   (The L3 module is now appearing)
!
#module 4 empty
!
#module 5 empty
!
#module 6 empty
end
Console> (enable)
Console> (enable) show module
Mod Slot Ports Module-Type              Model              Sub Status
--- ---- ----- ------------------------ ------------------ --- --------
1   1    2     1000BaseX Supervisor     WS-X4013           no  ok
3   3    34    Router Switch Card       WS-X4232-L3        no  ok

Mod Module-Name         Serial-Num
--- ------------------- --------------------
1                       JAB0442000Q9
3                       JAB044204L3

Mod MAC-Address(es)                         Hw     Fw          Sw
--- --------------------------------------- ------ ----------- -----------------
1   00-03-6b-a8-13-00 to 00-03-6b-a8-16-ff 1.2    5.4(1)      6.2(1)
3   00-01-96-d8-d9-ca to 00-01-96-d8-d9-eb 1.5    12.0(7)W5(  12.0(7)W5(15d)
Console> (enable)
```

Step 11

If you want to remove the old image from Flash, you need to use the **cd bootflash:** command to move to the bootflash directory. You can use the **dir** command to see the contents. Note that the output is a little different from that for the **show flash** command, shown earlier:

```
Console> cd bootflash:
Console> dir
-#- -length- -----date/time------ name
  1  3526384 --- -- ---- --:--:-- cat4000.5-4-2.bin
  2  4089736 Apr 17 2001 14:40:15 cat4000.6-2-1.bin

7981192 bytes available (7616376 bytes used)
```

Go to privileged mode and use the delete command to remove the file. Use the dir command to confirm that the file appears to be gone:

```
Console> enable

Enter password:

Console> (enable) delete cat4000.5-4-2.bin
Console> (enable) dir
-#- -length- -----date/time------ name
  2  4089736 Apr 17 2001 14:40:15 cat4000.6-2-1.bin

7981192 bytes available (7616376 bytes used)
```

Note that the "bytes available" and "bytes used" have not changed. The file is actually just hidden—much like deleting records in a database. To see the deleted file, use the dir deleted command. To remove the file, use the squeeze bootflash: command:

```
Console> (enable) dir deleted
-#- ED --type-- --crc--- -seek-- nlen -length- ----date/time---- name
  1 .. ffffffff 548c8f9c  39cf70   17  3526384 -- -- ---- --:-:- cat4000.5-4-2.bin

7981192 bytes available (7616376 bytes used)
Console> (enable) squeeze bootflash:

All deleted files will be removed, proceed (y/n) [n]? y

Squeeze operation may take a while, proceed (y/n) y
```

This should take less than two minutes:

```
Console> (enable) dir
-#- -length- -----date/time------ name
  1  4089736 Apr 17 2001 14:40:15 cat4000.6-2-1.bin

12070928 bytes available (4089736 bytes used)
```

Now you are done upgrading the CatOS image.

Lab 3-2: Catalyst 4000 Setup

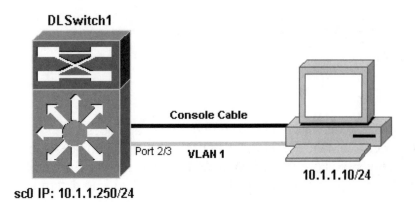

Objective

Configure a Cisco Catalyst 4000 Ethernet switch for the first time.

Scenario

You have just purchased a new Catalyst 4000 Ethernet switch with a Supervisor Engine II and a 32-port Layer 3 Services module. Use the command-line interface (CLI) to configure the Supervisor module so that it has a name, an in-band management IP address, and basic password security.

Step 1

Use a standard Cisco console (rollover) cable to connect the Catalyst 4000 console port to one of the workstation's serial ports via the Cisco RJ-45-to-DB9 serial adapter. You might notice that the Layer 3 Services module and the Supervisor module each have a console port. Because you are not configuring the L3 module, you plug into the Supervisor module console port.

Use the same communications settings that you use to connect to a router: 8 data bits, no parity, 1 stop bit, and no flow control.

Step 2

Power on the 4000 switch and observe the screen output as it boots:

```
WS-X4013 bootrom version 5.4(1), built on 2000.04.04 10:48:54
H/W Revisions:     Crumb: 5     Rancor: 8     Board: 2
Supervisor MAC addresses: 00:02:4b:59:30:00 through 00:02:4b:59:33:ff (1024 addresses)
Installed memory: 64 MB
Testing LEDs.... done!
...
```

It takes several minutes for the 4000 to boot up; the 4000 switch is much more verbose in its startup messages than Cisco routers are.

Step 3

As soon as the bootup is complete, you see a password prompt:

```
IP address for Catalyst not configured
DHCP/BOOTP will commence after the ports are online
Ports are coming online ...

Cisco Systems, Inc. Console

Enter password:
```

Because the switch has not been configured yet and does not have an IP address, the switch tries to obtain an address via DHCP. If the switch does gain an IP address from a DHCP server, you can use the command **show interface** from a console connection or use CDP information from a neighboring Cisco device to determine what address it obtained.

To log into the switch, press Enter at the password prompt. (The device ships with a null password.) You see the switch user EXEC prompt:

```
Console>
```

Step 4

Next, configure the switch name, user EXEC password, and privileged-mode password. To do this, you need to be in privileged mode:

```
Console> enable      (when prompted for a password, just press Enter)
Console(enable)>

Console(enable)> set system name DLSwitch1
System name set.
DLSwitch1(enable)>
```

With CatOS release 4.4 and later, if you use the **set system name** command to assign a name to the switch, the switch name is used as the prompt string and as the system name (as seen with the **show system** command). However, if you specify a different prompt string using the **set prompt** command, that string is used for the prompt, but the **set prompt** command does not affect the system name.

Setting the passwords requires that you enter a password setting dialog. This is different from other Cisco devices, where you type the password as part of the password command itself. The Catalyst 4000 has two passwords, just as Cisco IOS Software devices do. The first password is a user EXEC password, and the second is a privileged-mode password:

```
DLSwitch1(enable)> set password
Enter old password: (Because you do not currently have a password, press Enter.)
Enter new password:
Retype new password:
Password changed.
```

```
DLSwitch1(enable)> set enablepass
Enter old password: (Because you do not currently have a password, press Enter.)
Enter new password:
Retype new password:
Password changed.

DLSwitch1(enable)>
```

Step 5

Type **show config** to look at the switch's configuration:

```
This command shows non-default configurations only.
Use 'show config all' to show both default and non-default configurations.
.....
...............
..

begin
!
# ***** NON-DEFAULT CONFIGURATION *****
!
#time: Wed Nov 1 2000, 10:13:54 CST
!
#version 5.4(2)
!
set password $2$CBqb$emYj5ImVlOCgbNQTg.TC31
set enablepass $2$0o8Z$gGVzWMgEwfQEZIi2F340Q.
<output omitted>
```

The switch tells you that only nondefault commands are displayed. If all commands were displayed, the configuration would be very long. You have the **show config all** command option if you want to display the entire configuration.

Type **show config all** to see how big the configuration is.

1. What do you notice about the passwords that are stored in the configuration?

_____

2. Are they encrypted? _____

3. Did you have to do anything special to encrypt them?

_____

Step 6

Next, you configure the in-band management IP address on the switch so that you can communicate with the switch via the network for management purposes.

You see a port on the Supervisor module that is labeled 10/100 MGT. This is not a normal switch port, but rather an Ethernet interface that can administer the switch from an independent management network. This is sometimes called *out-of-band management*. This port would be connected to some other Ethernet network that is not part of your normal production network. If the Ethernet networks within this switch fail for some reason, you can still communicate with the switch through this external Ethernet interface. This out-of-band Ethernet port acts much like a NIC card on a workstation.

The 10/100 out-of-band management interface is called interface me1.

There is also a virtual interface inside the switch. This is a logical interface with no physical port associated with it. The sc0 interface is an in-band management interface that can be configured to be a member of any VLAN on the switch. The sc0 interface is connected to the switching fabric and participates in the functions of a normal switch port, such as spanning tree and CDP. The switching fabric is the hardware architecture that enables high-speed point-to-point connections to each line card.

You configure your management IP address on the sc0 virtual interface. By configuring the sc0 interface, you allow switch management to occur through the normal switch ports on the switch. You do not use the me1 interface in this lab:

```
DLSwitch1(enable) set interface sc0 10.1.1.250 255.255.255.0
```

You also configure the VLAN for which you want interface sc0 to be a member:

```
DLSwitch1(enable) set interface sc0 1
```

This places the virtual management interface in VLAN 1. By default, the sc0 interface is in VLAN 1, so this command is not necessary. However, it would be if you wanted to associate the management with a different VLAN.

Because this is a switch and not a router, you cannot configure any routing protocols on the Supervisor Engine II. However, on the Catalyst 4006 Supervisor Engine III, the route processor is built into the Supervisor Engine.

To ensure that you can reach all the networks that are a part of your internetwork, you need to configure a default router to send all traffic to when you are unsure of what path to take to get to the destination:

```
DLSwitch1(enable) set ip route default 10.1.1.1
```

This command installs a default route that points to the router with IP address 10.1.1.1.

Step 7

Configure your workstation with IP address 10.1.1.10/24. This IP address puts the workstation on the 10.1.1.0/24 management network.

Plug your workstation into port 2/3 with a straight-through cable. By default, all the ports in the switch are in VLAN 1, so as long as you left interface sc0 in VLAN 1, you should be able to communicate with the switch.

After the LED for port 2/3 turns green, telnet to the switch by using the IP address you configured for interface sc0: 10.1.1.250.

Log in using the password you configured. If you type **show vlan** at this point, you should see output for only VLAN 1.

Step 8

Using the Telnet connection, you can explore some of the switch **show** commands.

Type **show module** at the user EXEC prompt.

This command gives you information about the modules installed in the switch. Because the switch is a modular switch with removable blades (line cards), this display might vary. You also can see what hardware, firmware, and software each module is running. This is useful when you're determining which modules need to be upgraded:

```
DLSwitch1> show module
Mod Slot Ports Module-Type                  Model               Sub Status
--- ---- ----- ------------------------     ------------------  --- --------
1   1    2     1000BaseX Supervisor         WS-X4013            no  ok
2   2    34    Router Switch Card           WS-X4232-L3         no  ok

Mod Module-Name           Serial-Num
--- ------------------    --------------------
1                         JAB043402VU
2                         JAB04300JN8

Mod MAC-Address(es)                                    Hw     Fw          Sw
--- --------------------------------------------- ------ ---------- ------------------
1   00-03-6b-0b-7c-00 to 00-03-6b-0b-7f-ff 1.2     5.4(1)     5.5(1)
2   00-01-96-c8-e4-c6 to 00-01-96-c8-e4-e7 1.5     12.0(7)W5( 12.0(7)W5(15d)
```

Type **show system** at the user EXEC prompt.

This command gives you information about the switch's physical operation. It tells you the status of the power supplies, the status of the fans, the system uptime, and the percentage of current and peak traffic the switch has observed:

```
DLSwitch1> show system
PS1-Status PS2-Status PS3-Status PEM Installed
---------- ---------- ---------- -------------
ok         ok         none       no

Fan-Status Temp-Alarm Sys-Status Uptime d,h:m:s Logout
---------- ---------- ---------- -------------- ---------
ok         off        ok         1,00:52:12     20 min

PS1-Type     PS2-Type     PS3-Type
------------ ------------ ------------
WS-C4008     WS-C4008     none

Modem   Baud  Traffic Peak Peak-Time
```

```
------- ----- ------- ---- -------------------------
disable  9600   0%        0% Thu Nov 2 2000, 10:43:34

System Name                 System Location          System Contact          CC
----------------------      ----------------------   ----------------------- ---
<output omitted>
```

Type **show port** at the user EXEC prompt.

This command gives you the status of the ports that are installed on this switch. Based on what modules you installed, this display might vary:

```
DLSwitch1> show port
Port Name                   Status     Vlan         Level  Duplex Speed Type
----- ------------------    ---------- -----------  ------ ------ ----- -----------
1/1                         notconnect 1            normal full   1000  No GBIC
1/2                         notconnect 1            normal full   1000  No GBIC
2/1                         connected  1            normal full   1000  No GBIC
2/2                         connected  1            normal full   1000  No GBIC
2/3                         notconnect 1            normal auto   auto  10/100BaseTX
2/4                         notconnect 1            normal auto   auto  10/100BaseTX
2/5                         notconnect 1            normal auto   auto  10/100BaseTX
2/6                         notconnect 1            normal auto   auto  10/100BaseTX
2/7                         notconnect 1            normal auto   auto  10/100BaseTX
2/8                         notconnect 1            normal auto   auto  10/100BaseTX
2/9                         notconnect 1            normal auto   auto  10/100BaseTX
2/10                        notconnect 1            normal auto   auto  10/100BaseTX
<output omitted>
```

You now know how to set up a new CatOS switch for remote management.

Lab 3-3: Catalyst 2900 Setup

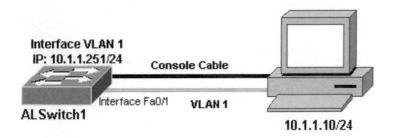

Objective

Configure a Cisco Catalyst 2900 XL Ethernet switch for the first time. The procedures used in this lab can also be used to configure a Catalyst 2950, 3500 XL, or 3550 switch.

Scenario

You just unpacked a Catalyst 2912 XL Ethernet switch. Configure the switch with a name, a management IP address, and basic password security using the CLI.

Step 1

Use a standard Cisco console (rollover) cable to connect the console port of the Catalyst 2900 XL to one of the workstation's serial ports via the Cisco RJ-45-to-DB9 serial adapter. The console port for the 2900 XL is located on the back of the switch, as it is on a Catalyst 1900 switch.

Use the same communications settings that you use to connect to a router: 8 data bits, no parity, 1 stop bit, and no flow control.

Step 2

For this lab, you want to simulate the configuration of a brand-new 2900 XL switch that has never been configured. If this is not the first time your 2900 XL switch has been used, in order to ensure that the lab steps proceed as described (simulating the Cisco IOS Software output seen on a 2900 XL switch right out of the box), go into privileged mode on the switch (just as you would on a Cisco router) and type the following commands in sequence: **erase start**, **delete vlan.dat**, and **reload**. The **delete vlan.dat** command is important for removing residual VLAN information on 2900 XL switches. If you don't type this command, the fact that your switch boots into the System Configuration dialog box does not mean that no residual VLAN information remains in Flash memory.

If you are working with a new 2900 XL switch, simply power it on.

In either case (after you type the four privileged-mode commands or power on a new switch), watch the output as the switch boots up:

```
C2900XL Boot Loader (C2900-HBOOT-M) Version 12.0(5)XU, RELEASE SOFTWARE (fc1)
          Compiled Mon 03-Apr-00 17:20 by swati
           starting...
          Base ethernet MAC Address: 00:02:b9:9a:85:80
          Xmodem file system is available.
          Initializing Flash...
          flashfs[0]: 108 files, 3 directories
          flashfs[0]: 0 orphaned files, 0 orphaned directories
          flashfs[0]: Total bytes: 3612672
          flashfs[0]: Bytes used: 2775040
          flashfs[0]: Bytes available: 837632
          flashfs[0]: flashfs fsck took 6 seconds.
          ...done Initializing Flash.
          Boot Sector Filesystem (bs:) installed, fsid: 3
          Parameter Block Filesystem (pb:) installed, fsid: 4
Loading "flash:c2900XL-c3h2s-mz-120.5-
XU.bin"...#####################################################
########################################################
#########################################
...
```

It takes a little more than 1 minute for the 2900 XL to boot up.

Step 3

After bootup is complete, you are prompted for the System Configuration dialog box. This is because you currently do not have a saved configuration on the switch:

```
IOS (tm) C2900XL Software (C2900XL-C3H2S-M), Version 12.0(5)XU,
  RELEASE SOFTWARE (fc1)
Copyright (c) 1986-2000 by cisco Systems, Inc.
Compiled Mon 03-Apr-00 16:37 by swati

        --- System Configuration Dialog ---

At any point you may type a question mark '?' for help.
Use ctrl-c to abort configuration dialog at any prompt.
Default settings are in square brackets '[]'.

Continue with configuration dialog? [yes/no] :
```

Answer **no**.

You will configure the switch manually without the assistance of the setup dialog box. The setup dialog box is much simpler than that for a Cisco router. After you complete this lab, reconfigure the switch using the System Configuration dialog box.

You are not prompted for a password. Your switch is placed directly in user EXEC mode:

```
Switch>
```

Step 4

Take a look at the current default running configuration before you add any configuration commands. You need to move to privileged mode to display the configuration. Because you have not configured an enable password yet, you are not prompted for one. Proceed as follows:

```
Switch>enable
Switch#show running-config

Building configuration...

Current configuration:
!
version 12.0
no service pad
service timestamps debug uptime
service timestamps log uptime
no service password-encryption
!
hostname Switch
!
ip subnet-zero
!
interface FastEthernet0/1
!
interface FastEthernet0/2
!
interface FastEthernet0/3
!
interface FastEthernet0/4
!
interface FastEthernet0/5
!
interface FastEthernet0/6
!
interface FastEthernet0/7
!
interface FastEthernet0/8
!
interface FastEthernet0/9
!
interface FastEthernet0/10
!
interface FastEthernet0/11
!
interface FastEthernet0/12
!
interface VLAN1
 no ip directed-broadcast
 no ip route-cache
!
!
line con 0
 transport input none
 stopbits 1
line vty 5 15
!
end
```

Notice that the configuration is like that for a Cisco router. The Fast Ethernet interfaces displayed in the configuration are actually switch ports. Also notice the lack of any Layer 3 options, such as routing protocols (this is not a multilayer switch). On a Catalyst 3550 with the Enhanced Image, you have the option of configuring Layer 3 features such as routing protocols and interface IP addresses; with the 3550 switch, you have the option of configuring an interface as a Layer 2 switch port or as a Layer 3 routed port.

Step 5

Next, you configure the switch name, user EXEC password, and privileged-mode password.

A Catalyst 2900 XL uses Cisco router-style configuration commands, so these commands will all look quite familiar:

```
Switch>enable
Switch#
```

Set the switch name:

```
Switch#config terminal
Switch(config)#hostname ALSwitch
ALSwitch(config)#
```

Set the passwords:

```
ALSwitch(config)#enable secret class
ALSwitch(config)#line console 0
ALSwitch(config-line)#password cisco
ALSwitch(config-line)#login
ALSwitch(config-line)#line vty 0 15
ALSwitch(config-line)#password cisco
ALSwitch(config-line)#login
```

To save the configuration, you must copy the running configuration to the startup configuration, exactly as you would on a Cisco router. With the CatOS, such as on a Catalyst 6500 switch, the configuration file is automatically updated each time a command is typed, as shown here:

```
ALSwitch#copy running-config startup-config
```

Step 6

Now, you configure the management IP address on the switch so that you can communicate with the switch over the network.

The 2900 XL series switches default to using VLAN 1 as their network management interface. The running-config output shows **interface vlan 1** as part of the default configuration.

Because all ports default to membership in VLAN 1, you configure your switch management to also use VLAN 1. You configure interface VLAN 1 just like you configure a router interface when assigning the switch's management IP address:

```
ALSwitch#configure terminal
ALSwitch(config)#interface vlan 1
ALSwitch(config-if)#ip address 10.1.1.251 255.255.255.0
```

This immediately assigns the switch's IP address to VLAN 1 (the management VLAN). You can change the management VLAN for the 2900 XL to VLAN *x* by creating another switch virtual interface (SVI) with the command **interface VLAN** *x*, but only one management VLAN can be administratively active at a time. On the Catalyst 3550, you enable inter-VLAN routing by creating an SVI for each VLAN you want to route for. In this case, you need to make sure that each VLAN interface (SVI) has an IP address on that VLAN's subnet.

Because the 2900 XL is not a multilayer switch, you cannot configure any routing protocols on this device. To ensure that you can reach all the networks that are a part of your internetwork, you need to configure a default router to send all traffic to when you are unsure of what path to take to get to the destination:

```
ALSwitch(config)#ip default-gateway 10.1.1.1
```

This command installs a default route that points to the router with IP address 10.1.1.1.

Step 7

Configure your workstation with IP address 10.1.1.10/24 so that it is part of the network management subnet: 10.1.1.0/24.

Plug your workstation into interface Fa0/1. By default, all the ports in the switch are in VLAN 1, so as long as you configured your management IP address on VLAN 1, you should be able to communicate with the switch.

Telnet to the switch by using the management IP address you configured for the switch (10.1.1.251).

Log in using the password you configured (cisco). If you type the command **show vlan**, you see output for only VLAN 1.

Step 8

Using the Telnet connection, you can explore some of the commands on the 2900 XL. Use the **show interfaces** command to look at the status of the switch's interfaces. Notice that the command output is similar to that for a Cisco router:

```
ALSwitch#show interfaces
FastEthernet0/1 is down, line protocol is down
  Hardware is Fast Ethernet, address is 0002.fd49.7b81
    (bia 0002.fd49.7b81)
  MTU 1500 bytes, BW 0 Kbit, DLY 100 usec,
    reliability 255/255, txload 1/255, rxload 1/255
```

```
Encapsulation ARPA, loopback not set
Keepalive not set
Auto-duplex , Auto Speed , 100BaseTX/FX
ARP type: ARPA, ARP Timeout 04:00:00
Last input never, output never, output hang never
Last clearing of "show interface" counters never
Queueing strategy: fifo
Output queue 0/40, 0 drops; input queue 0/75, 0 drops
5 minute input rate 0 bits/sec, 0 packets/sec
5 minute output rate 0 bits/sec, 0 packets/sec
   1 packets input, 64 bytes
   Received 0 broadcasts, 0 runts, 0 giants, 0 throttles
   0 input errors, 0 CRC, 0 frame, 0 overrun, 0 ignored
   0 watchdog, 0 multicast
   0 input packets with dribble condition detected
   1 packets output, 64 bytes, 0 underruns
   0 output errors, 0 collisions, 1 interface resets
   0 babbles, 0 late collision, 0 deferred
   0 lost carrier, 0 no carrier
<output omitted>
```

1. What other types of interfaces do you see in addition to the switch ports?

_____

_____

Type **show version** to view the hardware and software information:

```
ALSwitch#show version
Cisco Internetwork Operating System Software
IOS (tm) C2900XL Software (C2900XL-C3H2S-M), Version 12.0(5)XU, RELEASE SOFTWARE
 (fc1)
Copyright (c) 1986-2000 by cisco Systems, Inc.
Compiled Mon 03-Apr-00 16:37 by swati
Image text-base: 0x00003000, data-base: 0x00301398

ROM: Bootstrap program is C2900XL boot loader

ALSwitch uptime is 16 minutes
System returned to ROM by power-on
System image file is "flash:c2900XL-c3h2s-mz-120.5-XU.bin"


cisco WS-C2924-XL (PowerPC403GA) processor (revision 0x11) with 8192K/1024K bytes of memory.
Processor board ID 0x0E, with hardware revision 0x01
Last reset from power-on

Processor is running Enterprise Edition Software
Cluster command switch capable
Cluster member switch capable
24 FastEthernet/IEEE 802.3 interface(s)

32K bytes of flash-simulated non-volatile configuration memory.
Base ethernet MAC Address: 00:02:FD:49:7B:80
Motherboard assembly number: 73-3382-08
Power supply part number: 34-0834-01
Motherboard serial number: FAB04301ANJ
Power supply serial number: PHI04150042
Model revision number: A0
Motherboard revision number: B0
Model number: WS-C2924-XL-EN
```

```
System serial number: FAB0432S2GJ
Configuration register is 0xF

ALSwitch#
```

2. What type of memory is included in the Catalyst 2900 XL series switch but is not listed in the **show version** output?

_____

Lab 3-4: Catalyst 4000 Password Recovery

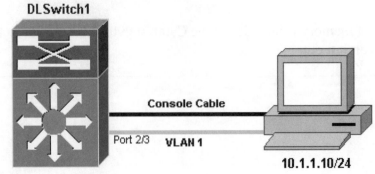

Objective

Regain control of a Cisco Catalyst 4000 switch running CatOS after you lost the passwords.

Scenario

You take a job at a company that uses Catalyst 4000 switches for the network's distribution layer. The person who previously managed the network left abruptly and did not leave any documentation containing the passwords. Perform password recovery on the Catalyst 4000 switch, changing the normal-mode password to "cisco" and the privileged-mode password to "class."

Step 1

Configure your 4000 switch according to the diagram. First, you configure the system name:

```
Console> enable
Console> (enable)> set system name DLSwitch1
System name set.
DLSwitch1> (enable)
```

Have someone set the passwords, as in the following steps. Tell whomever sets the passwords not to use the standard passwords but to make up some of his own. Make sure he does not tell you what passwords he sets:

```
DLSwitch1> (enable) set password
Enter old password: (Because you do not currently have a password, press Enter.)
Enter new password:
Retype new password:
Password changed.

DLSwitch1> (enable) set enablepass
Enter old password: (Because you do not currently have a password, press Enter.)
Enter new password:
Retype new password:
Password changed.
```

Configure the sc0 interface with IP address 10.1.1.250/24 and as a member of VLAN 1:

```
DLSwitch1> (enable) set interface sc0 10.1.1.250 255.255.255.0
DLSwitch1> (enable) set interface sc0 1
```

Configure your workstation's IP address as 10.1.1.10/24.

Step 2

Attempt to telnet into the Catalyst switch. You cannot get in because you do not know the passwords.

A Catalyst 4000 series switch handles password recovery differently than Cisco IOS Software-based devices.

In short, a Catalyst 4000 series switch does not require a password when you log in from the console port during the first 30 seconds after it has booted up. A password is still required during this time if you are trying to log in via Telnet.

This is a great example of why the physical security of your devices is so important. Anyone who can get access to your console port will have the ability to change your passwords.

Step 3

Make sure you are connected to the console port of the Catalyst 4000 switch. Power off your switch (unplug the two power cords). Read through the rest of this step because you need to complete it within 30 seconds after the switch begins displaying output. It is important to disconnect the power to your switch because a warm reset doesn't let you perform password recovery.

Power on your Catalyst 4000 switch (plug in the two power cords).

Watch the startup messages. As soon as you see the following, press Enter immediately (remember that you do not need a password to log in):

```
Cisco Systems, Inc. Console

Enter password:

DLSwitch1>
```

Type privileged mode. You do not need a password; just press Enter:

```
DLSwitch1> enable
DLSwitch1> (enable)
```

Now you reset the passwords using the **set password** and **set enablepass** commands. As when you log in, when prompted for the current passwords, press Enter:

```
DLSwitch1> (enable) set password
Enter old password:      (Press Enter)
Enter new password:      (Enter "cisco")
Retype new password:     (Enter "cisco" again)
Password changed.

DLSwitch1> (enable) set enablepass
Enter old password:      (Press Enter)
Enter new password:      (Enter "class")
Retype new password:     (Enter "class" again)
Password changed.
```

Your password recovery is now complete.

Your new passwords are now part of the saved configuration. The rest of the switch's configuration is unchanged.

1. Why is the Catalyst 4000 CatOS password recovery better or worse than that of Cisco IOS Software-based devices?

_____

_____

_____

_____

_____

_____

_____

_____

_____

_____

Lab 3-5: Catalyst 2900 Password Recovery

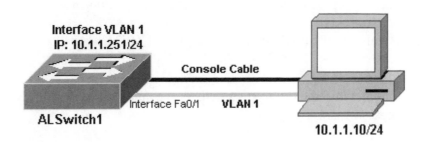

Objective

Regain control of a Cisco Catalyst 2900 XL switch after you lost the passwords. The technique demonstrated also applies to Catalyst 2950, 3500 XL, and 3550 switches.

Scenario

You take a job at a company that uses Catalyst 2900 XL switches in its intermediate distribution facilities (IDFs). The person who previously managed the network left abruptly and did not leave any documentation containing the passwords. Perform password recovery on the Catalyst 2900 XL, changing the console and vty line passwords to "cisco" and the enable secret password to "class."

Step 1

First, configure your 2900 XL switch according to the diagram. You can also use the configuration from Lab 3-3 and skip this step:

```
Switch>enable
Switch#


Switch#configure terminal
Switch(config)#hostname ALSwitch
ALSwitch(config)#
```

Have someone set the passwords, as shown in the following steps. Tell him to not use the standard passwords but to make up some of his own. Make sure he does not tell you what passwords he sets.

```
ALSwitch(config)#enable secret somethingdifferent
ALSwitch(config)#line console 0
ALSwitch(config-line)#password somethingelse
ALSwitch(config-line)#login
ALSwitch(config-line)#line vty 0 15
ALSwitch(config-line)#password somethingelse
ALSwitch(config-line)#login
```

Configure the virtual management interface, interface VLAN 1, with IP address 10.1.1.251/24:

```
ALSwitch(config)#interface vlan 1
ALSwitch(config-if)#ip address 10.1.1.251 255.255.255.0
```

Configure your workstation's IP address as 10.1.1.10/24.

Step 2

Attempt to telnet into the Catalyst switch. You cannot get in, because you do not know the passwords.

The Catalyst 2900 XL switch handles password recovery in a fashion similar to other Cisco IOS Software-based devices. The idea is to circumvent the current startup-config so that the switch loads the default configuration, which has no passwords. As soon as the switch is up and running, you type enable mode, copy the startup-config to the running-config, modify the passwords, and then save the startup-config.

Although the idea is the same, the way you go about it is a little different than with a Cisco router.

Step 3

Make sure you are connected to the console port, and power off your Catalyst 2900 XL switch.

Hold down the MODE button on the front of the Catalyst 2900 XL switch at the same time you power on the switch. You can let go of the MODE button a second or two after the LED light above port 1 is no longer lit.

Watch the startup messages. When you see the **switch:** prompt, type **flash_init** followed by **load_helper**:

```
C2900XL Boot Loader (C2900-HBOOT-M) Version 12.0(5)XU, RELEASE SOFTWARE (fc1)
Compiled Mon 03-Apr-00 17:20 by swati
 starting...
Base ethernet MAC Address: 00:02:b9:9a:85:80
Xmodem file system is available.

The system has been interrupted prior to initializing the
flash filesystem.  The following commands will initialize
the flash filesystem, and finish loading the operating
system software:

    flash_init
    load_helper
    boot

switch:


switch:flash_init
Initializing Flash...
```

```
flashfs[0]: 109 files, 3 directories
flashfs[0]: 0 orphaned files, 0 orphaned directories
flashfs[0]: Total bytes: 3612672
flashfs[0]: Bytes used: 2776064
flashfs[0]: Bytes available: 836608
flashfs[0]: flashfs fsck took 8 seconds.
...done Initializing Flash.
Boot Sector Filesystem (bs:) installed, fsid: 3
Parameter Block Filesystem (pb:) installed, fsid: 4
switch:load_helper
```

What you are doing here is similar to changing the config-register on a router to boot into ROM monitor mode.

List the contents of the switch's Flash memory:

```
switch:dir flash:
Directory of flash:/

2     -rwx  1644046  <date>        c2900XL-c3h2s-mz-120.5-XU.bin
3     -rwx  105961   <date>        c2900XL-diag-mz-120.5-XU
4     drwx  6784     <date>        html
111   -rwx  286      <date>        env_vars
112   -rwx  648      <date>        config.text

836608 bytes available (2776064 bytes used)
```

The file config.text contains your startup-config. You want to rename this file to a temporary file, config.old, as shown here:

```
switch:rename flash:config.text flash:config.old
```

Now reboot the switch:

```
Switch:reboot
```

When the switch reboots, it prompts you to enter the Configuration dialog box. Answer **no** when asked whether you want to continue with the Configuration dialog.

When the switch finishes the boot sequence, type privileged mode, and rename the temporary file with the original filename:

```
Switch>
Switch>enable
Switch#rename flash:config.old flash:config.text
```

Copy the startup-config (config.text) to your running-config:

```
Switch#copy flash:config.text system:running-config
Destination filename [running-config]?  (Press Enter)
648 bytes copied in 1.206 secs (648 bytes/sec)
ALSwitch#
```

Because you are currently in privileged mode, you can reassign the passwords and save the configuration:

```
ALSwitch(config)#enable secret class
ALSwitch(config)#line console 0
ALSwitch(config-line)#password cisco
ALSwitch(config-line)#loginALSwitch(config-line)#line vty 0 15
ALSwitch(config-line)#password cisco
ALSwitch(config-line)#login
ALSwitch(config-line)#end
ALSwitch#copy running-config startup-config
```

Your password change is now complete.

Note: Password recovery procedures for all Cisco devices can be conveniently accessed from the web site www.cisco.com/warp/public/474/index.shtml.

Lab 3-6: Catalyst 4000 TFTP Configuration Files

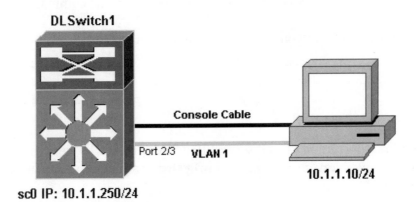

DLSwitch1

Console Cable

Port 2/3   **VLAN 1**

10.1.1.10/24

sc0 IP: 10.1.1.250/24

Objective

Copy your current configuration to a TFTP server.

Scenario

You take a job at a company that uses Catalyst 4000 switches in the distribution layer. You want to save a copy of the configuration file from a Catalyst 4000 switch to a TFTP server for backup.

Step 1

Configure your 4000 switch according to the diagram. If you want, you can use the same configuration you used in Lab 3-4 and skip this step. First, you configure the system name, the normal- and privileged-mode passwords, and the management interface:

```
Console> enable
Console(enable)> set system name DLSwitch1
System name set.
DLSwitch1(enable)>

DLSwitch1(enable)> set password
Enter old password: (Because you do not currently have a password, press Enter.)
Enter new password:
Retype new password:
Password changed.

DLSwitch1(enable)> set enablepass
Enter old password: (Because you do not currently have a password, press Enter.)
Enter new password:
Retype new password:
Password changed.

DLSwitch1(enable) set interface sc0 10.1.1.250 255.255.255.0
DLSwitch1(enable) set interface sc0 1
```

Configure your workstation's IP address as 10.1.1.10/24. The workstation acts as the TFTP server. Make sure the Cisco TFTP server is loaded on the workstation.

Step 2

Use the **copy** command to copy the configuration from the switch to the TFTP server. Type **copy ?** to see which options are available for this command.

1. What other locations can you copy the configuration file to?

_____

_____

_____

Step 3

Ping the workstation (TFTP server) IP address 10.1.1.10 from the switch to confirm connectivity. Now, use the **copy config tftp** command to copy the configuration to your TFTP server:

```
DLSwitch1> (enable) copy config tftp
This command uploads non-default configurations only.
Use 'copy config tftp all' to upload both default and non-default configurations.
IP address or name of remote host []? 10.1.1.10
Name of file to copy to [DLSwitch1.cfg]?        (Just press Enter.)

Upload configuration to tftp:DLSwitch1.cfg, (y/n) [n]? y
.....


  . .
   -

Configuration has been copied successfully.
DLSwitch1> (enable)
```

Step 4

Check the configuration file that was saved to your TFTP server.

2. Is the copy a full version of the configuration or just the nondefault commands?

_____

_____

3. What command would you use to save both default and nondefault commands?

_____

_____

Lab 3-7: Catalyst 2900 TFTP Configuration Files

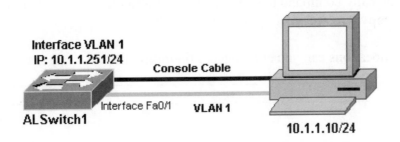

Objective

The objective of this lab is to copy your current configuration to a TFTP server. The procedure demonstrated here also works on Catalyst 2950, 3500 XL, and 3550 switches.

Scenario

You take a job at a company that uses Catalyst 2900 XL switches in its IDFs. You want to save a copy of the configuration file from your Catalyst 2900 XL switch to a TFTP server for backup.

Step 1

Configure your 2900 XL switch according to the diagram. If you want, you can use the same configuration you used in Lab 3-5 and skip this step. First, you configure the switch name, the enable secret password, the console and vty line passwords, and the management interface:

```
Switch>enable
Switch#

Switch#configure terminal
Switch(config)#hostname ALSwitch
ALSwitch(config)#

ALSwitch(config)#enable secret class
ALSwitch(config)#line console 0
ALSwitch(config-line)#password cisco
ALSwitch(config-line)#login
ALSwitch(config-line)#line vty 0 15
ALSwitch(config-line)#password cisco
ALSwitch(config-line)#login

ALSwitch(config)#interface vlan 1
ALSwitch(config-if)#ip address 10.1.1.251 255.255.255.0
```

Configure your workstation's IP address as 10.1.1.10/24. The workstation acts as the TFTP server. Make sure you have the Cisco TFTP server loaded on the workstation.

Step 2

Use the **copy** command to copy the configuration from the switch to the TFTP server. Type **copy ?** to see what options are available.

1. What other locations can you copy the configuration file to?

_____

_____

Step 3

Ping the workstation (TFTP server) IP address 10.1.1.10 from the switch to confirm connectivity. Now use the **copy running-config tftp** command to copy the configuration file to your TFTP server:

```
ALSwitch#copy running-config tftp
Address or name of remote host []? 10.1.1.10
Destination filename [running-config]? ALSwitch (Use your switch name.)
!!
1165 bytes copied in 4.173 secs (291 bytes/sec)
ALSwitch#
```

Step 4

Check the configuration file that was saved to your TFTP server.

2. Is the copy a full version of the configuration, or just the non-default commands?

_____

Lab 4-1: Catalyst 4000 Static VLANs

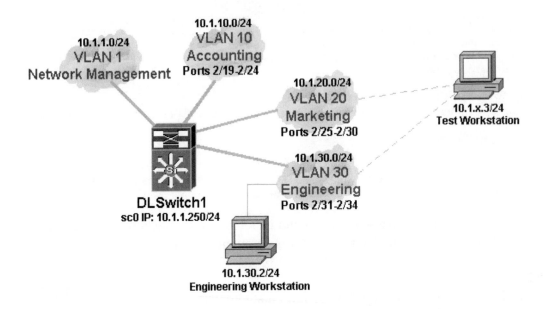

Objective

Configure your access layer Catalyst 4000 switch to support the four VLANs: Marketing, Accounting, Engineering, and Network Management.

Scenario

You are migrating your current hub-based network to a Catalyst 4000 switch-based network. You currently have three hubs, one for each network. You need to create three VLANs on your new switch in addition to the existing default VLAN. You must assign specific ports to each VLAN.

Design

VLAN port assignments:

VLANs	VLAN 1 Network Management	VLAN 10 Accounting	VLAN 20 Marketing	VLAN 30 Engineering
Port Number	3–18	19–24	25–30	31–34

Step 1

Configure your Catalyst 4000 switch with a name and an in-band management IP address, as shown in the diagram. If you want, you can use the same configuration you used in Lab 3-6 and skip this step. First, you configure the system name, the normal- and privileged-mode passwords, and the management interface:

```
Console> enable
  Console> (enable) set system name DLSwitch1
```

```
System name set.
DLSwitch1> (enable)

DLSwitch1> (enable) set password
Enter old password: (Because you don't currently have a password, press Enter.)
Enter new password:
Retype new password:
Password changed.

DLSwitch1> (enable) set enablepass
Enter old password: (Because you don't currently have a password, press Enter.)
Enter new password:
Retype new password:
Password changed.

DLSwitch1> (enable) set interface sc0 10.1.1.250 255.255.255.0
DLSwitch1> (enable) set interface sc0 1
```

Note: The **set interface sc0 1** command is not necessary because interface sc0 is in VLAN 1 by default. I've included this command for emphasis.

Step 2

Before you configure the VLANs, you must understand a little about the default operation of the Catalyst 4000.

By default, the Catalyst 4000 is configured as a VTP (VLAN Trunk Protocol) server. You learn more about VTP in Labs 4-3 and 4-4. Before creating new VLANs, you must assign the switch a VTP domain name:

```
DLSwitch1> (enable) set vtp domain corp
```

This command sets the VTP server domain name to "corp", which is what you will be using for the remaining labs. The VTP domain name is case-sensitive.

Step 3

Assign ports to the appropriate VLANs, according to the network diagram.

Use the **set vlan 10** {*vlans*}{*mod/ports*} command to assign the ports to the appropriate VLANs:

```
DLSwitch1> (enable) set vlan 10 2/19-24
```

Notice that you can specify multiple ports by indicating a range of port numbers. **2/19-24** includes ports 19 through 24 on module 2.

The switch returns a confirmation of the VLAN assignment:

```
Vlan 10 configuration successful
VLAN 10 modified.
VLAN 1 modified.
VLAN  Mod/Ports
----  ----------------------
10    2/19-24
```

1. Why does the switch tell you that VLAN 1 was modified?

_____

_____

Configure the appropriate ports to be members of VLANs 20 and 30:

```
DLSwitch1> (enable) set vlan 20 2/25-30
DLSwitch1> (enable) set vlan 30 2/31-34
```

By default, you do not need to configure the other ports to be members of VLAN 1 because VLAN 1 is the default VLAN that ports are automatically assigned to.

Use the **show vlan** command to verify that your ports are assigned to the correct VLAN.

2. What is the maximum number of VLANs supported on a Catalyst 4000 switch?

_____

Step 4

Configure the Engineering workstation for the Engineering VLAN using the IP address 10.1.30.2/24. Make sure the Engineering workstation is plugged into one of the Engineering VLAN ports.

3. What ports are connected to the Engineering VLAN? _____

4. What command can you use to determine the ports assigned to a given VLAN?

_____

You can assign names to your VLANs so that they are easier to identify when you use **show** commands on the switch. These names are simply labels; they do not affect the VLANs' functionality:

```
DLSwitch1> (enable) set vlan 10 name Accounting
DLSwitch1> (enable) set vlan 20 name Marketing
DLSwitch1> (enable) set vlan 30 name Engineering
```

Execute another **show vlan** command:

```
DLSwitch> (enable) show vlan
VLAN Name                             Status    IfIndex Mod/Ports, Vlans
---- -------------------------------- --------- ------- ----------------------
1    default                          active    6       1/1-2
                                                        2/1-18
10   Accounting                       active    45      2/19-24
20   Marketing                        active    46      2/25-30
30   Engineering                      active    47      2/31-34
1002 fddi-default                     active    7
1003 token-ring-default               active    10
1004 fddinet-default                  active    8
1005 trnet-default                    active    9
```

Step 5

Configure the Test workstation so that it has an IP address of 10.1.20.3/24, and plug it into the Marketing VLAN.

5. What ports are in the Marketing VLAN? _____

6. Can you ping 10.1.30.2, the IP address of the Engineering workstation? _____

7. What is needed for you to be able to ping the Engineering workstation?

_____

Step 6

Change the IP address of the Test workstation to 10.1.30.3/24.

8. Can you ping the Engineering workstation now? _____

If you can't ping the Engineering workstation after you changed the IP address, make sure you moved the Test workstation to the Engineering VLAN after changing the IP address.

This lab showed you how to configure VLAN names and VLAN port membership for Catalyst 4000 switches. You learned how to display VLAN information and how to use the **ping** command on workstations to test for inter-VLAN and intra-VLAN connectivity.

Lab 4-2: Catalyst 2900 Static VLANs

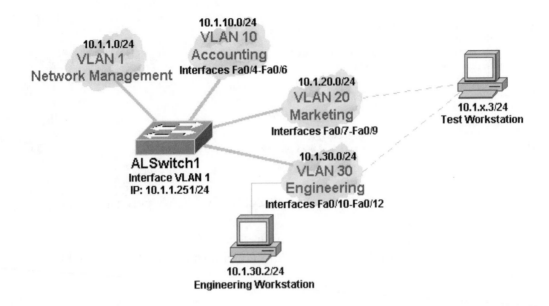

Objective

Configure your access layer Catalyst 2900 XL switch to support the four VLANs: Marketing, Accounting, Engineering, and Network Management.

Scenario

You are migrating your current hub-based network to a Catalyst 2900 XL switch-based network. You currently have three hubs, one for each network. You must create three VLANs on your new switch (in addition to the existing default VLAN) and assign three ports to each of these VLANs.

Design

VLAN port/interface assignments:

VLANs	VLAN 1 Network Management	VLAN 10 Accounting	VLAN 20 Marketing	VLAN 30 Engineering
Port Number	Fa0/1–Fa0/3	Fa0/4–Fa0/6	Fa0/7–Fa0/9	Fa0/10–Fa0/12

Step 1

Configure your 2900 switch according to the diagram with a name and an in-band management IP address. If you like, you can use the same configuration you used in Lab 3-7 and skip this step. First, you configure the switch name, the enable secret password, the console and vty line passwords, and the management interface:

```
Switch>enable
Switch#
```

```
Switch#configure terminal
Switch(config)#hostname ALSwitch
ALSwitch(config)#

ALSwitch(config)#enable secret class
ALSwitch(config)#line console 0
ALSwitch(config-line)#password cisco
ALSwitch(config-line)#login
ALSwitch(config-line)#line vty 0 15
ALSwitch(config-line)#password cisco
ALSwitch(config-line)#login

ALSwitch(config)#interface vlan 1
ALSwitch(config-if)#ip address 10.1.1.250 255.255.255.0
```

Step 2

Configure the VLANs. Refer to the Design section for VLAN port assignments.

The Catalyst 2900 XL switch will be configured as a VTP client. In Lab 4-3, the 2900 XL switch will learn VLAN information over a trunk link from the VTP server (Catalyst 4000).

To configure the VTP domain name and the VLAN names, enter VLAN configuration mode by using the privileged-mode command **vlan database** on the 2900 XL switch:

```
ALSwitch#vlan database
ALSwitch(vlan)#vtp client
ALSwitch(vlan)#vtp domain corp
ALSwitch(vlan)#vlan 10 name Accounting
ALSwitch(vlan)#vlan 20 name Marketing
ALSwitch(vlan)#vlan 30 name Engineering
ALSwitch(vlan)#exit
ALSwitch#
```

Also, you need to configure all the ports as access ports. A port on a 2900 XL switch can be an access port or a trunk port. You use trunk ports when connecting a switch to a switch or to another device that understands VLAN trunking. Because you will only be connecting workstations to the switch ports, you need to configure these ports as access ports, which means that they will be single VLAN ports with standard devices attached.

By default, all ports are configured as access ports, so the following command is not necessary. Normally, it is used only if interface Fa0/1 was set up previously as a trunk port:

```
ALSwitch(config)#interface fa0/1
ALSwitch(config-if)#switchport mode access
```

You must repeat this step for all ports that need to be converted back to access ports.

1. What command(s) could you use to determine if a port is in access or trunk mode?

_____

Step 3

Next, you assign ports to their appropriate VLANs. Use the **switchport access vlan** *n* command, where *n* is the VLAN number, to assign ports to the appropriate VLANs:

```
ALSwitch(config)#interface fa0/4
ALSwitch(config-if)#switchport access vlan 10

ALSwitch(config)#interface fa0/5
ALSwitch(config-if)#switchport access vlan 10

ALSwitch(config)#interface fa0/6
ALSwitch(config-if)#switchport access vlan 10

ALSwitch(config)#interface fa0/7
ALSwitch(config-if)#switchport access vlan 20

ALSwitch(config)#interface fa0/8
ALSwitch(config-if)#switchport access vlan 20

ALSwitch(config)#interface fa0/9
ALSwitch(config-if)#switchport access vlan 20

ALSwitch(config)#interface fa0/10
ALSwitch(config-if)#switchport access vlan 30

ALSwitch(config)#interface fa0/11
ALSwitch(config-if)#switchport access vlan 30

ALSwitch(config)#interface fa0/12
ALSwitch(config-if)#switchport access vlan 30
```

By default, you do not need to configure interface Fa0/1–Fa0/3 for VLAN 1 because VLAN 1 is the default VLAN to which ports are assigned.

If you are using a Catalyst 2950 with Cisco IOS Software Release 12.1(6)EA2 or later, or if you are using a Catalyst 3550 switch with Cisco IOS Software Release 12.1(4)EA1 or later, you can get the same effect as with the preceding commands by using the **interface range** command. For example, you would enter the command **interface range fastethernet0/4 -6** (the space after the **4** is required) to enter interface range configuration mode, followed by the command **switchport access vlan 10**.

Use the **show vlan** command to verify that your ports are assigned to the correct VLANs.

2. What is the maximum number of VLANs supported on a Catalyst 2900 XL switch?

_____

Step 4

Configure the Engineering workstation to be on the Engineering VLAN with the IP address 10.1.30.2/24. Make sure the Engineering workstation is plugged into one of the Engineering VLAN ports.

3. What ports are connected to the Engineering VLAN? _____

4. What command can you use to determine which ports are assigned to a given VLAN?
_____

Step 5

Configure the Test workstation so that it has an IP address of 10.1.20.3/24, and connect the workstation to the Marketing VLAN.

5. What ports are in the Marketing VLAN? _____

6. Can you ping 10.1.30.2, the IP address of the Engineering workstation? _____

7. What is needed for you to be able to ping the Engineering workstation?
_____
_____

Step 6

Change the IP address of the Test workstation to 10.1.30.3/24.

8. Can you ping the Engineering workstation now? _____

If you can't ping the Engineering workstation after you changed the IP address, make sure you moved the Test workstation to the Engineering VLAN after changing the IP address.

This lab showed you how to configure static VLANs on a 2900 XL switch. The procedures demonstrated here also apply to Catalyst 2950, 3500 XL, and 3550 switches. You also used the **ping** command on workstations to test intra-VLAN and inter-VLAN connectivity.

Lab 4-3: VLAN Trunking and VTP Domains

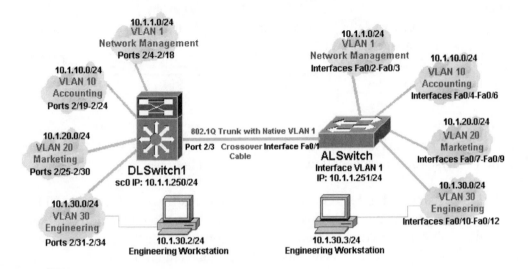

Objective

Configure a VLAN trunk between a Catalyst 4000 switch and a Catalyst 2900 XL switch. This procedure also works when the Catalyst 2900 XL switch is replaced by a Catalyst 2950, 3500 XL, or 3550 switch.

Scenario

Your network is growing. You have outgrown your 2900 XL, and you need to add more port capacity. As time goes on, your plan is to continue adding Catalyst 2900 XL switches in your intermediate distribution facilities (IDFs). At this point, you are adding a Catalyst 4000 in your main distribution facility (MDF) to interconnect all the 2900 XL switches. To make your network easier to manage when it comes to additions, moves, and changes, you are configuring VLANs throughout your entire network. The 4000 switch will reside at the core of this topology.

You need to configure the link between the 4000 switch and the 2900 XL switch as a trunk link that extends the configured VLANs to span the network. The 4000 switch will act as a VLAN Trunk Protocol (VTP) server that will propagate VLAN information to the 2900 XL switch, which will act as a VTP client.

Design

Switched network VTP configuration information:

Switch	VTP Domain	VTP Mode
DLSwitch1	corp	server
ALSwitch	corp	client

VLAN port assignments:

Switch	VLAN 1 Network Management	VLAN 10 Accounting	VLAN 20 Marketing	VLAN 30 Engineering
DLSwitch1	4–18	19–24	25–30	31–34
ALSwitch	2–3	4–6	7–9	10–12

Step 1

Clear the configurations and residual VLAN information on both the Catalyst 2900 XL and Catalyst 4006 switches. Power-cycle the switches.

Configure the name and in-band management IP address for your Catalyst 4000 switch according to the diagram. If you want, you can use the same configuration you used in Lab 4-1 and skip this step. First, you configure the system name, the normal- and privileged-mode passwords, and the management interface:

```
Console> enable
Console> (enable) set system name DLSwitch1
System name set.
DLSwitch1> (enable)

DLSwitch1> (enable) set password
Enter old password: (Because you do not currently have a password, press Enter.)
Enter new password:
Retype new password:
Password changed.

DLSwitch1> (enable) set enablepass
Enter old password: (Because you do not currently have a password, press Enter.)
Enter new password:
Retype new password:
Password changed.

DLSwitch1> (enable) set interface sc0 10.1.1.250 255.255.255.0
DLSwitch1> (enable) set interface sc0 1
```

Step 2

Configure your 2900 XL switch name and in-band management IP address according to the network diagram. If you want, you can use the same configuration you used in Lab 4-2 and skip this step. You configure the switch name, the enable secret password, the console and vty line passwords, and the management interface:

```
Switch> enable
Switch#

Switch#configure terminal
Switch(config)#hostname ALSwitch
ALSwitch(config)#

ALSwitch(config)#enable secret class
ALSwitch(config)#line console 0
```

```
ALSwitch(config-line)#password cisco
ALSwitch(config-line)#login
ALSwitch(config-line)#line vty 0 15
ALSwitch(config-line)#password cisco
ALSwitch(config-line)#login

ALSwitch(config)#interface vlan 1
ALSwitch(config-if)#ip address 10.1.1.251 255.255.255.0
```

Step 3

You need to configure VTP on both switches. VTP is the protocol that communicates VLAN information between switches. If VTP did not provide this
information, you would have to manually create the VLANs on every switch.

By default, the Catalyst 4000 switch is configured as a VTP server.

Because the switch defaults to a VTP server, no configuration is necessary. In the
event that the switch was not configured as a VTP server, the following command
configures the switch as a VTP server:

```
DLSwitch1> (enable) set vtp mode server
```

You want the 4000 switch to act as a VTP server to provide VLAN information to
the other switches. As soon as the 4000 switch is set up as a VTP server, you need
to specify the VTP domain name, as shown here:

```
DLSwitch1> (enable) set vtp domain corp
```

This command sets the VTP server domain name to "corp." This name must match
all other switches in the VTP domain. The VTP domain name is case-sensitive.

The Catalyst 2900 XL switch will be configured as a VTP client. You want the
2900 XL switch to learn the VLANs from the VTP server.

You do this with the **vlan database** command on a 2900 XL switch. This command
puts you in VLAN configuration mode. Note that you enter this mode from the
privileged EXEC mode prompt, not global configuration mode:

```
ALSwitch#vlan database
ALSwitch(vlan)#vtp client
ALSwitch(vlan)#vtp domain corp
ALSwitch(vlan)#exit
ALSwitch#
```

This sets the 2900 XL switch in VTP client mode and sets the VTP domain name to
"corp." Note that the 2900 XL would learn the VTP domain name from the 4006
switch (without your entering the command **vtp domain corp** on the 2900 XL) if
the 2900 XL switch were configured as a VTP client, the 4006 switch were
configured as a VTP server, and the trunk between the switches were active.

As soon as VTP is configured, you are ready to configure the VLANs.

Step 4

Assign ports on the 4000 switch to the appropriate VLANs, and configure names for each VLAN:

```
DLSwitch1> (enable) set vlan 10 2/19-24
DLSwitch1> (enable) set vlan 20 2/25-30
DLSwitch1> (enable) set vlan 30 2/31-34
DLSwitch1> (enable) set vlan 10 name Accounting
DLSwitch1> (enable) set vlan 20 name Marketing
DLSwitch1> (enable) set vlan 30 name Engineering
```

By default, you do not need to configure the other ports for VLAN 1 because that is the default VLAN to which ports are assigned.

Use the **show vlan** command to verify that your ports are assigned to the correct VLAN:

```
DLSwitch1> (enable) show vlan
VLAN Name                             Status    IfIndex Mod/Ports, Vlans
---- -------------------------------- --------- ------- --------------------------
1    default                          active    6       1/1-2
                                                        2/1-18
10   Accounting                       active    45      2/19-24
20   Marketing                        active    46      2/25-30
30   Engineering                      active    47      2/31-34
1002 fddi-default                     active    7
1003 token-ring-default               active    10
1004 fddinet-default                  active    8
1005 trnet-default                    active    9
```

Because the 2900 XL switch is in VTP client mode, all this VLAN information should get passed on to the 2900 XL from the 4000 switch.

Step 5

Now you can cable the trunk line (if you haven't already). Connect interface Fa0/1 on ALSwitch to port 2/3 (the first 10/100 Ethernet port) on the L3 module of DLSwitch1.

1. What kind of cable do you need to use when you connect two switches with UTP cable? _____

Use the appropriate cable to connect these two switches.

Step 6

Configure each end of the trunk link with 802.1Q trunk encapsulation.

On the Catalyst 4000, use the following:

```
DLSwitch1> (enable) set trunk 2/3 nonegotiate dot1q 1-1005
```

This command sets port 2/3 to an 802.1Q trunk that supports VLANs 1 to 1005. The **nonegotiate** keyword tells the switch that it should not try to autonegotiate what type of trunk link this is (because the 2900 XL on the other end does not support autonegotiation, and both sides must support autonegotiation for it to work).

On the Catalyst 2900 XL, use the following:

```
ALSwitch#configure terminal
ALSwitch(config)#interface fa0/1
ALSwitch(config-if)#switchport mode trunk
ALSwitch(config-if)#switchport trunk encapsulation dot1q
```

The first interface command tells the switch that this switch port is a trunk port. The second command tells the switch to use 802.1Q trunk encapsulation.

Step 7

Now that the VLAN trunk link is configured, you need to check to see if your VTP client (the 2900 XL) has learned of the defined VLANs.

You might need to give the two switches a few moments to exchange VLAN information.

Use the **show vlan** command on the 2900 XL to see if it has learned the new VLANs from the 4000 switch:

```
ALSwitch#show vlan
VLAN Name                             Status    Ports
---- -------------------------------- --------- -------------------------------
1    default                          active    Fa0/2, Fa0/3, Fa0/4, Fa0/5,
                                                Fa0/6, Fa0/7, Fa0/8, Fa0/9,
                                                Fa0/10, Fa0/11, Fa0/12

10   Accounting                       active
20   Marketing                        active
30   Engineering                      active
1002 fddi-default                     active
1003 token-ring-default               active
1004 fddinet-default                  active
1005 trnet-default                    active

VLAN Type  SAID       MTU   Parent RingNo BridgeNo Stp  BrdgMode Trans1 Trans2
---- ----- ---------- ----- ------ ------ -------- ---- -------- ------ ------
1    enet  100001     1500  -      -      -        -    -        0      0
10   enet  100010     1500  -      -      -        -    -        0      0
20   enet  100020     1500  -      -      -        -    -        0      0
30   enet  100030     1500  -      -      -        -    -        0      0
1002 fddi  101002     1500  -      0      -        -    -        0      0
1003 tr    101003     1500  -      0      -        -    srb      0      0
1004 fdnet 101004     1500  -      -      -        ieee -        0      0
1005 trnet 101005     1500  -      -      -        ibm  -        0      0
```

You should now see the three VLANs on the 2900 XL that were created on the 4000 switch.

Even though the VLANs are now configured on the 2900 XL, you have not assigned any ports to them yet.

Step 8

Assign ports on the 2900 XL to the appropriate VLANs:

```
ALSwitch(config)#interface fa0/4
ALSwitch(config-if)#switchport access vlan 10

ALSwitch(config)#interface fa0/5
ALSwitch(config-if)#switchport access vlan 10

ALSwitch(config)#interface fa0/6
ALSwitch(config-if)#switchport access vlan 10

ALSwitch(config)# interface fa0/7
ALSwitch(config-if)#switchport access vlan 20

ALSwitch(config)#interface fa0/8
ALSwitch(config-if)#switchport access vlan 20

ALSwitch(config)#interface fa0/9
ALSwitch(config-if)#switchport access vlan 20

ALSwitch(config)#interface fa0/10
ALSwitch(config-if)#switchport access vlan 30

ALSwitch(config)#interface fa0/11
ALSwitch(config-if)#switchport access vlan 30

ALSwitch(config)#interface fa0/12
ALSwitch(config-if)#switchport access vlan 30
```

If you are using a Catalyst 2950 with Cisco IOS Software Release 12.1(6)EA2 or later, or if you are using a Catalyst 3550 switch with Cisco IOS Software Release 12.1(4)EA1 or later, you can achieve the same effect as with the previous commands by using the **interface range** command. For example, you would enter the command **interface range fastethernet0/4 -6** (the space after the **4** is required) to enter interface range configuration mode, followed by the command **switchport access vlan 10**.

Step 9

On the Catalyst 2900 XL, examine the output of the **show vtp counters** and **show vtp status** commands.

2. What command shows how many VTP advertisements have been transmitted and received?

_____

_____

3. What command shows which VTP mode (server or client) the switch is in?

_____

Step 10

On the Catalyst 4000 switch, examine the output of the **show vtp statistics** and **show vtp domain** commands.

4. What command shows how many VTP advertisements have been transmitted and received?

_____

5. What command shows which VTP mode (server or client) the switch is in?

_____

Step 11

Place one workstation in the Engineering VLAN on the Catalyst 4000 switch with IP address 10.1.30.2/24. Place another workstation in the Engineering VLAN on the 2900 XL switch with IP address 10.1.30.3/24. Try to ping between the workstations. The ping should be successful.

Lab 4-4: VTP Pruning

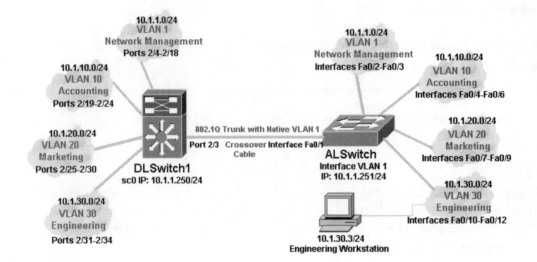

Objective

Configure VTP pruning in a VTP domain consisting of a Catalyst 4000 switch and Catalyst 2900 XL switches.

Scenario

You have configured a VTP trunk line between your distribution layer switch and your access layer switch. No workstations in VLANs 10 and 20 are connected to your access layer switch. So, there is no reason for broadcast traffic for VLANs 10 and 20 to travel over the trunk link and down to the access layer.

VTP pruning allows VTP to intelligently determine if there are no devices in a particular VLAN at the other end of a trunk link and temporarily prune that VLAN from the trunk. If an access layer device joins that VLAN, the VLAN is reenabled on the trunk.

Design

Switched network VTP configuration information:

Switch	VTP Domain	VTP Mode
DLSwitch1	corp	server
ALSwitch	corp	client

VLAN port assignments:

Switch	VLAN 1 Network Management	VLAN 10 Accounting	VLAN 20 Marketing	VLAN 30 Engineering
DLSwitch1	4–18	19–24	25–30	31–34
ALSwitch	2–3	4–6	7–9	10–12

Note: If you are continuing from the VTP trunk and VTP domain lab (Lab 4-3), you can skip to Step 10.

Step 1

Clear the configurations and residual VLAN information on both the Catalyst 2900 XL and Catalyst 4006 switches. Power-cycle the switches.

Configure the name and in-band management IP address for your Catalyst 4000 switch according to the diagram. If you want, you can use the same configuration you used in Lab 4-1 and skip this step. First, you configure the system name, the normal- and privileged-mode passwords, and the management interface:

```
Console> enable
Console> (enable) set system name DLSwitch1
System name set.
DLSwitch1> (enable)

DLSwitch1> (enable) set password
Enter old password: (Because you do not currently have a password, press Enter.)
Enter new password:
Retype new password:
Password changed.

DLSwitch1> (enable) set enablepass
Enter old password: (Because you do not currently have a password, press Enter.)
Enter new password:
Retype new password:
Password changed.

DLSwitch1> (enable) set interface sc0 10.1.1.250 255.255.255.0
DLSwitch1> (enable) set interface sc0 1
```

Step 2

Configure your 2900 XL switch name and in-band management IP address according to the network diagram. If you want, you can use the same configuration you used in Lab 4-2 and skip this step. You configure the switch name, the enable secret password, the console and vty line passwords, and the management interface:

```
Switch> enable
Switch#

Switch#configure terminal
Switch(config)#hostname ALSwitch
```

```
ALSwitch(config)#
ALSwitch(config)#enable secret class
ALSwitch(config)#line console 0
ALSwitch(config-line)#password cisco
ALSwitch(config-line)#login
ALSwitch(config-line)#line vty 0 15
ALSwitch(config-line)#password cisco
ALSwitch(config-line)#login

ALSwitch(config)#interface vlan 1
ALSwitch(config-if)#ip address 10.1.1.251 255.255.255.0
```

Step 3

You need to configure VTP on both switches. VTP is the protocol that communicates VLAN information between switches. If VTP did not provide this information, you would have to manually create the VLANs on every switch.

By default, the Catalyst 4000 switch is configured as a VTP server.

Because the switch defaults to a VTP server, no configuration is necessary. If the switch were not configured as a VTP server, the following command would do so:

```
DLSwitch1> (enable) set vtp mode server
```

You want the 4000 switch to act as a VTP server to provide VLAN information to the other switches. After you have set up the 4000 switch as a VTP server, you need to specify the VTP domain name, as shown here:

```
DLSwitch1> (enable) set vtp domain corp
```

This command sets the VTP server domain name to "corp." This name must match all other switches in the VTP domain. The VTP domain name is case-sensitive.

The Catalyst 2900 XL switch will be configured as a VTP client. You want the 2900 XL switch to learn the VLANs from the VTP server.

You do this with the **vlan database** command on a 2900 XL switch. This command puts you in VLAN configuration mode. Note that you enter this mode from the privileged EXEC mode prompt, not the global configuration mode:

```
ALSwitch#vlan database
ALSwitch(vlan)#vtp client
ALSwitch(vlan)#vtp domain corp
ALSwitch(vlan)#exit
ALSwitch#
```

This sets the 2900 XL switch in VTP client mode and sets the VTP domain name to "corp." Note that the 2900 XL would learn the VTP domain name from the 4006 switch (without your entering the command **vtp domain corp** on the 2900 XL) if the 2900 XL switch were configured as a VTP client, the 4006 switch were configured as a VTP server, and the trunk between the switches were active.

As soon as VTP is configured, you are ready to configure the VLANs.

Step 4

Next, you assign ports on the 4000 switch to the appropriate VLANs and configure names for each VLAN:

```
DLSwitch1> (enable) set vlan 10 2/19-24
DLSwitch1> (enable) set vlan 20 2/25-30
DLSwitch1> (enable) set vlan 30 2/31-34
DLSwitch1> (enable) set vlan 10 name Accounting
DLSwitch1> (enable) set vlan 20 name Marketing
DLSwitch1> (enable) set vlan 30 name Engineering
```

By default, you do not need to configure the other ports for VLAN 1, because that is the default VLAN to which ports are assigned.

Use the **show vlan** command to verify that your ports are assigned to the correct VLANs:

```
DLSwitch1> (enable) show vlan
VLAN Name                             Status    IfIndex Mod/Ports, Vlans
---- -------------------------------- --------- ------- ------------------------
1    default                          active    6       1/1-2
                                                        2/1-18
10   Accounting                       active    45      2/19-24
20   Marketing                        active    46      2/25-30
30   Engineering                      active    47      2/31-34
1002 fddi-default                     active    7
1003 token-ring-default               active    10
1004 fddinet-default                  active    8
1005 trnet-default                    active    9
```

Because the 2900 XL switch is in VTP client mode, all this VLAN information should get passed on to the 2900 XL from the 4000 switch.

Step 5

Now you can cable the trunk line (if you haven't already). Connect interface Fa0/1 on ALSwitch to port 2/3 (the first 10/100 Ethernet port) on the L3 module of DLSwitch1. You assume here that the L3 module is in slot 2 of the 4006 chassis.

1. What kind of cable do you need to use when you connect two switches with UTP cable? _____

Use the appropriate cable to connect these two switches.

Step 6

Configure each end of the trunk link with 802.1Q trunk encapsulation.

On the Catalyst 4000, use the following:

```
DLSwitch1> (enable) set trunk 2/3 nonegotiate dot1q 1-1005
```

This command sets port 2/3 to an 802.1Q trunk that supports VLANs 1 to 1005. The **nonegotiate** keyword tells the switch that it should not try to autonegotiate what type of trunk link this is (because the 2900 XL on the other end does not support autonegotiation, and both sides must support autonegotiation for it to work).

On the Catalyst 2900 XL, use the following:

```
ALSwitch#configure terminal
ALSwitch(config)#interface fa0/1
ALSwitch(config-if)#switchport mode trunk
ALSwitch(config-if)#switchport trunk encapsulation dot1q
```

The first interface command tells the switch that this switch port is a trunk port. The second command tells the switch to use 802.1Q trunk encapsulation.

Step 7

Now that the VLAN trunk link is configured, you need to check to see if your VTP client (the 2900 XL) has learned of the defined VLANs.

You might need to give the two switches a few moments to exchange VLAN information.

Use the **show vlan** command on the 2900 XL to see if it has learned of the new VLANs from the 4000 switch:

```
ALSwitch#show vlan
VLAN Name                             Status    Ports
---- -------------------------------- --------- -------------------------------
1    default                          active    Fa0/2, Fa0/3, Fa0/4, Fa0/5,
                                                 Fa0/6, Fa0/7, Fa0/8, Fa0/9,
                                                 Fa0/10, Fa0/11, Fa0/12
10   Accounting                       active
20   Marketing                        active
30   Engineering                      active
1002 fddi-default                     active
1003 token-ring-default               active
1004 fddinet-default                  active
1005 trnet-default                    active

VLAN Type  SAID       MTU   Parent RingNo BridgeNo Stp  BrdgMode Trans1 Trans2
---- ----- ---------- ----- ------ ------ -------- ---- -------- ------ ------
1    enet  100001     1500  -      -      -        -    -        0      0
10   enet  100010     1500  -      -      -        -    -        0      0
20   enet  100020     1500  -      -      -        -    -        0      0
30   enet  100030     1500  -      -      -        -    -        0      0
1002 fddi  101002     1500  -      0      -        -    -        0      0
1003 tr    101003     1500  -      0      -        -    srb      0      0
1004 fdnet 101004     1500  -      -      -        ieee -        0      0
1005 trnet 101005     1500  -      -      -        ibm  -        0      0
```

You should now see the three VLANs on the 2900 XL that were created on the 4000 switch.

Although the VLANs are now configured on the 2900 XL, you have not assigned any ports to the VLANs yet.

Step 8

Assign ports on the 2900 XL to the appropriate VLANs:

```
ALSwitch(config)#interface fa0/4
ALSwitch(config-if)#switchport access vlan 10

ALSwitch(config)#interface fa0/5
ALSwitch(config-if)#switchport access vlan 10

ALSwitch(config)#interface fa0/6
ALSwitch(config-if)#switchport access vlan 10

ALSwitch(config)# interface fa0/7
ALSwitch(config-if)#switchport access vlan 20

ALSwitch(config)#interface fa0/8
ALSwitch(config-if)#switchport access vlan 20

ALSwitch(config)#interface fa0/9
ALSwitch(config-if)#switchport access vlan 20

ALSwitch(config)#interface fa0/10
ALSwitch(config-if)#switchport access vlan 30

ALSwitch(config)#interface fa0/11
ALSwitch(config-if)#switchport access vlan 30

ALSwitch(config)#interface fa0/12
ALSwitch(config-if)#switchport access vlan 30
```

If you are using a Catalyst 2950 with Cisco IOS Software Release 12.1(6)EA2 or later, or if you are using a Catalyst 3550 switch with Cisco IOS Software Release 12.1(4)EA1 or later, you can achieve the same effect as with the previous commands by using the **interface range** command. For example, you would enter the command **interface range fastethernet0/4 -6** (the space after the **4** is required) to enter interface range configuration mode, followed by the command **switchport access vlan 10**.

Step 9

From ALSwitch, attempt to ping DLSwitch1. You should be successful:

```
ALSwitch#ping 10.1.1.250

Type escape sequence to abort.
Sending 5, 100-byte ICMP Echos to 10.1.1.250, timeout is 2 seconds:
!!!!!
Success rate is 100 percent (5/5), round-trip min/avg/max = 6/13/36 ms
```

Step 10

Make sure that no devices are plugged into the nontrunk ports on ALSwitch. If the Engineering workstation is plugged into VLAN 30 of the 2900 XL switch, as shown in the diagram, unplug it.

Examine the output from the **show trunk** command on DLSwitch1:

```
DLSwitch1> (enable) show trunk
* - indicates vtp domain mismatch
Port       Mode          Encapsulation  Status         Native vlan
--------   -----------   -------------  ------------   -----------
 2/3       nonegotiate   dot1q          trunking       1

Port       Vlans allowed on trunk
--------   ---------------------------------------------------------------------
 2/3       1-1005

Port       Vlans allowed and active in management domain
--------   ---------------------------------------------------------------------
 2/3       1,10,20,30

Port       Vlans in spanning tree forwarding state and not pruned
--------   ---------------------------------------------------------------------
 2/3       1,10,20,30
```

Notice that all defined VLANs 10, 20, and 30 are in "spanning tree forwarding state and not pruned." But there are no devices on ALSwitch. It would be a shame to forward broadcast traffic for VLANs 10, 20, and 30 if there are no devices in these VLANs to receive the traffic!

Step 11

VTP pruning solves this problem. VTP pruning checks the other end of a trunk link to see if there are any members in a VLAN. If there are not, then it "prunes" them from the spanning tree forwarding state. This temporarily keeps traffic for that VLAN from traversing the trunk link.

On DLSwitch1, use the following:

```
DLSwitch1> (enable) set vtp pruning enable
This command will enable the pruning function in the entire management domain.
All devices in the management domain should be pruning-capable before enabling.
Do you want to continue (y/n) [n]? y
```

On ALSwitch, use the following:

```
ALSwitch#vlan database
ALSwitch(vlan)#vtp pruning
ALSwitch(vlan)#exit
```

Note: It is sufficient to enable VTP pruning on just the 4006 switch. Enabling VTP pruning on a VTP server enables pruning for the entire management domain.

That's all there is to it. VTP pruning is now enabled.

Step 12

Verify that you are pruning:

```
DLSwitch1> (enable) show trunk
* - indicates vtp domain mismatch
Port        Mode          Encapsulation  Status        Native vlan
--------    -----------   -------------  ------------  -----------
 2/3        nonegotiate   dot1q          trunking      1

Port        Vlans allowed on trunk
--------    ----------------------------------------------------------------
 2/3        1-1005

Port        Vlans allowed and active in management domain
--------    ----------------------------------------------------------------
 2/3        1,10,20,30

Port        Vlans in spanning tree forwarding state and not pruned
--------    ----------------------------------------------------------------
 2/3        1
```

Notice that now, only VLAN 1 is in a forwarding state.

2. Why is VLAN 1 forwarding?

_____

_____

3. Why are none of the other VLANs forwarding?

_____

_____

Plug a workstation into a VLAN 30 port on ALSwitch, as shown in the diagram.

4. Check the **show trunk** command again. What changed?

_____

_____

Move your workstation to a port in either VLAN 10 or 20.

5. Does the spanning tree forwarding state update? If so, how long does it take to update?

_____

_____

Lab 5-1: Spanning-Tree Protocol Default Behavior

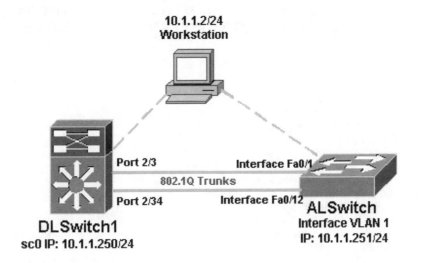

Objective

Observe the default behavior of Spanning-Tree Protocol (STP).

Scenario

You just finished installing two switches: one distribution layer Catalyst 4000 switch and one access layer Catalyst 2900 XL switch. You have redundant uplinks between the two switches. Because of the possibility of a bridge loop, spanning tree blocks data traffic on one of the links. In this lab, you observe STP's default behavior.

Step 1

First, configure the passwords, name, and in-band management IP address for your Catalyst 4000 switch according to the diagram. If you like, you can use the same configuration you used in Lab 4-1, "Catalyst 4000Static VLANs" and skip this step.

```
Console> enable
Console> (enable) set system name DLSwitch1
System name set.
DLSwitch1> (enable)

DLSwitch1> (enable) set password
Enter old password:      (Because you do not currently have a password, press Enter.)
Enter new password:
Retype new password:
Password changed.

DLSwitch1> (enable) set enablepass
Enter old password:      (Because you do not currently have a password, press Enter.)
Enter new password:
Retype new password:
Password changed.

DLSwitch1> (enable) set interface sc0 10.1.1.250 255.255.255.0
DLSwitch1> (enable) set interface sc0 1
```

Step 2

Configure your 2900 XL switch name, passwords, and in-band management IP address according to the diagram. If you like, you can use the same configuration you used in Lab 4-2, "Catalyst 2900 Static VLANs" and skip this step:

```
Switch> enable
Switch#


Switch#configure terminal
Switch(config)#hostname ALSwitch
ALSwitch(config)#

ALSwitch(config)#enable password class
ALSwitch(config)#line console 0
ALSwitch(config-line)#password cisco
ALSwitch(config-line)#login
ALSwitch(config-line)#line vty 0 15
ALSwitch(config-line)#password cisco
ALSwitch(config-line)#login

ALSwitch(config)#interface vlan 1
ALSwitch(config-if)#ip address 10.1.1.251 255.255.255.0
```

Step 3

Connect an uplink cable from port 2/3 on DLSwitch1 to interface Fa0/1 on ALSwitch. Connect an uplink cable from port 2/34 on DLSwitch1 to interface Fa0/12 on ALSwitch. Remember to use crossover cables.

As soon as you connect the cables and the links are detected, spanning tree goes into effect.

By default, spanning tree runs on every active port. That means that, when a new link becomes active, the port goes through the Listening, Learning, and Forwarding states before the link becomes active. During this discovery period, the first switch determines whether it is connected to another switch or to an end-user device.

In the event that the first switch detects another switch, the two switches begin building a spanning tree. The two switches elect a root bridge for the spanning tree and then agree on which links to keep active and which links to disable.

1. What type of frame does spanning tree use to communicate with other switches?

You might notice that, regardless of which order you install the uplinks in, the cable connecting port 2/3 to interface Fa0/1 becomes the active link.

Depending on which side of the link is blocking (the 2900 XL or the 4000 switch), you might have a difficult time reading the lights. In Blocking state, the 2900 XL changes its light to a distinct yellow color. The 4000 switch, on the other hand, has very small port lights; if the 4000 switch side of the link is blocked, you might have a hard time viewing the lights. You can always use the **show spantree** command on the 4000 switch to view the port status (here DLSwitch1 is the root):

```
DLSwitch1> (enable) show spantree
VLAN 1
Spanning tree enabled
Spanning tree type         ieee

Designated Root            00-02-4b-21-36-c0
Designated Root Priority   32768
Designated Root Cost       19
Designated Root Port       2/3
Root Max Age   20 sec   Hello Time 2  sec   Forward Delay 15 sec

Bridge ID MAC ADDR         00-02-4b-59-40-00
Bridge ID Priority         32768
Bridge Max Age 20 sec   Hello Time 2  sec   Forward Delay 15 sec

Port                   Vlan Port-State    Cost  Priority Portfast   Channel_id
---------------------- ---- ------------- ----- -------- ---------- ----------
<output omitted>
 2/3                   1    forwarding    19          32 disabled   0
<output omitted>
 2/34                  1    blocking      19          32 disabled   0
```

Notice that port 2/34 is blocking.

You can use the **show spanning-tree** command on ALSwitch to view the spanning tree status for the trunk ports (here, ALSwitch is the root):

```
ALSwitch#show spanning-tree

Spanning tree 1 is executing the IEEE compatible Spanning Tree protocol
  Bridge Identifier has priority 32768, address 0002.4b21.36c0
  Configured hello time 2, max age 20, forward delay 15
  We are the root of the spanning tree
  Topology change flag not set, detected flag not set, changes 5
  Times:  hold 1, topology change 35, notification 2
          hello 2, max age 20, forward delay 15
  Timers: hello 0, topology change 0, notification 0
  Fast uplink switchover is enabled

Interface Fa0/1 (port 13) in Spanning tree 1 is FORWARDING
  Port path cost 19, Port priority 128
  Designated root has priority 32768, address 0002.4b21.36c0
  Designated bridge has priority 32768, address 0002.4b21.36c0
  Designated port is 13, path cost 0
  Timers: message age 0, forward delay 0, hold 0
  BPDU: sent 2089, received 45

Interface Fa0/12 (port 25) in Spanning tree 1 is BLOCKING
  Port path cost 19, Port priority 128
  Designated root has priority 32768, address 0002.4b21.36c0
  Designated bridge has priority 32768, address 0002.4b21.36c0
  Designated port is 25, path cost 0
  Timers: message age 0, forward delay 0, hold 0
  BPDU: sent 3222, received 42
```

Notice that interface Fa0/12 is blocking.

The switch puts port 2/34 or interface Fa0/12 in Blocking state because it detects two links between the same switch. This would result in a bridge loop if the switches did not put one of the trunk ports in Blocking state.

Step 4

Assume that DLSwitch1 is blocking the backup link. Let's look at the spanning-tree output on the two switches:

```
DLSwitch1> (enable) show spantree
VLAN 1
Spanning tree enabled
Spanning tree type              ieee

Designated Root                 00-02-4b-21-36-c0
Designated Root Priority        32768
Designated Root Cost            19
Designated Root Port            2/3
Root Max Age    20 sec      Hello Time 2  sec   Forward Delay 15 sec

Bridge ID MAC ADDR              00-02-4b-59-40-00
Bridge ID Priority              32768
Bridge Max Age 20 sec       Hello Time 2  sec   Forward Delay 15 sec

Port                    Vlan Port-State   Cost  Priority Portfast   Channel_id
----------------------- ---- ------------ ----- -------- ---------- ----------
 2/3                     1    forwarding    19        32 disabled   0
<output omitted>
 2/34                    1    blocking      19        32 disabled   0

ALSwitch#show spanning-tree

Spanning tree 1 is executing the IEEE compatible Spanning Tree protocol
  Bridge Identifier has priority 32768, address 0002.4b21.36c0
  Configured hello time 2, max age 20, forward delay 15
  We are the root of the spanning tree
  Topology change flag not set, detected flag not set, changes 5
  Times:  hold 1, topology change 35, notification 2
          hello 2, max age 20, forward delay 15
  Timers: hello 0, topology change 0, notification 0
  Fast uplink switchover is enabled

Interface Fa0/1 (port 13) in Spanning tree 1 is FORWARDING
   Port path cost 19, Port priority 128
   Designated root has priority 32768, address 0002.4b21.36c0
   Designated bridge has priority 32768, address 0002.4b21.36c0
   Designated port is 13, path cost 0
   Timers: message age 0, forward delay 0, hold 0
   BPDU: sent 2089, received 45

Interface Fa0/12 (port 25) in Spanning tree 1 is FORWARDING
   Port path cost 19, Port priority 128
   Designated root has priority 32768, address 0002.4b21.36c0
   Designated bridge has priority 32768, address 0002.4b21.36c0
   Designated port is 25, path cost 0
   Timers: message age 0, forward delay 0, hold 0
   BPDU: sent 3222, received 42
```

By looking at the spanning-tree output from the two switches, answer these questions.

2. Which switch is the root of the spanning tree?

_____

3. How can you tell which switch is the root bridge?

_____

4. Why is that switch selected as the root bridge?

_____

5. What causes the backup link between port 2/34 and interface Fa0/12 to be blocked, as opposed to the active link between port 2/3 and interface Fa0/1?

_____

6. What causes the backup link to get blocked on the Catalyst 4000 side of the link rather than the Catalyst 2900 XL side of the link?

_____

In this example, you watch spanning tree's default operation. You do not specify any bridge priorities, so the switch with the lowest MAC address is elected root bridge. You do not specify any link priorities, so STP uses the port number to determine each trunk port's STP state. The lowest port number on the nonroot bridge is used as the root port for this particular topology.

In the Lab 5-2, "Root Bridges and Root Path Cost," you modify some of the STP priorities to alter STP's default behavior.

Challenge

Cross your uplink cables so that port 2/3 now connects to interface Fa0/12 and port 2/34 connects to interface Fa0/1.

Can you predict what will happen?

Think about how STP determines whether to put a port in Blocking state.

7. What port will be blocking?

_____

Now let's observe how spanning tree works with end-user devices.

First, connect a workstation to any of the unused switch ports on either switch. Power off your workstation. Now, power on the workstation. You will notice that the switch port turns yellow when the operating system initializes the NIC. The port is active, but the spanning-tree process is incomplete. As the PC boots, watch the color of the link light on the switch. You will observe that the PC makes it through most of the boot process before the link turns green (active). It should take about 30 seconds for a port connected to a workstation to become active.

8. Why does it take 30 seconds for the light to become green?

_____

_____

9. Why is it necessary for spanning tree to go through these steps on every port?

_____

_____

_____

Bridge loops can easily bring down a switched network. Spanning tree ensures that bridge loops are avoided in switched networks.

In the next lab, you modify STP priorities to alter spanning tree's default behavior. Save the configurations so that you can use them for the next lab.

Lab 5-2: Root Bridges and Root Path Cost

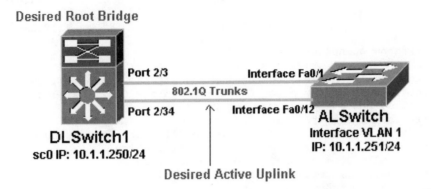

Objective

Modify spanning tree's default behavior to prescribe the root bridge and the active uplink.

Scenario

You are unhappy with spanning tree's default behavior. Your access layer switch has become the root bridge, and you prefer that your distribution layer switch serve this function. Also, you decide to use port priorities to control which links are elected as the active links.

In this lab, you learn about STP parameters that can be used to control how a spanning tree is constructed.

Step 1

Use the configuration from Lab 5-1. Make sure your uplink cables are connected as shown in the diagram.

Step 2

This lab assumes that DLSwitch1 is blocking the backup link. Here is the spanning-tree output for the two switches:

```
DLSwitch1> (enable) show spantree
VLAN 1
Spanning tree enabled
Spanning tree type          ieee

Designated Root             00-02-4b-21-36-c0
Designated Root Priority    32768
Designated Root Cost        19
Designated Root Port        2/3
Root Max Age   20 sec    Hello Time 2  sec    Forward Delay 15 sec

Bridge ID MAC ADDR          00-02-4b-59-40-00
Bridge ID Priority          32768
Bridge Max Age 20 sec    Hello Time 2  sec    Forward Delay 15 sec
```

```
Port                    Vlan Port-State     Cost  Priority Portfast   Channel_id
----------------------- ---- -------------- ----- -------- ---------- -----------
 2/3                    1    forwarding     19          32 disabled   0
<output omitted>
 2/34                   1    blocking       19          32 disabled   0
```

ALSwitch#**show spanning-tree**

```
Spanning tree 1 is executing the IEEE compatible Spanning Tree protocol
  Bridge Identifier has priority 32768, address 0002.4b21.36c0
  Configured hello time 2, max age 20, forward delay 15
  We are the root of the spanning tree
  Topology change flag not set, detected flag not set, changes 5
  Times:  hold 1, topology change 35, notification 2
          hello 2, max age 20, forward delay 15
  Timers: hello 0, topology change 0, notification 0
  Fast uplink switchover is enabled

Interface Fa0/1 (port 13) in Spanning tree 1 is FORWARDING
  Port path cost 19, Port priority 128
  Designated root has priority 32768, address 0002.4b21.36c0
  Designated bridge has priority 32768, address 0002.4b21.36c0
  Designated port is 13, path cost 0
  Timers: message age 0, forward delay 0, hold 0
  BPDU: sent 2089, received 45

Interface Fa0/12 (port 25) in Spanning tree 1 is FORWARDING
  Port path cost 19, Port priority 128
  Designated root has priority 32768, address 0002.4b21.36c0
  Designated bridge has priority 32768, address 0002.4b21.36c0
  Designated port is 25, path cost 0
  Timers: message age 0, forward delay 0, hold 0
  BPDU: sent 3222, received 42
```

Currently, ALSwitch is the root bridge, and the active link between the two switches is the link between port 2/3 and interface Fa0/1. Depending on your switches, your DLSwitch1 might be the root bridge.

You want to modify this behavior so that DLSwitch1 is the root bridge and the link between port 2/34 and interface Fa0/12 is the active link between the two switches.

Step 3

Set the bridge priority.

Remember that the root bridge is determined by selecting the switch with the lowest Bridge ID (BID). The BID is an 8-byte value consisting of an ordered pair of numbers. The first is a 2-byte decimal number called the bridge priority, and the second is a 6-byte (hexadecimal) MAC address. The possible values for bridge priority range between 0 and 65,535. The default setting is 32,768. The MAC address in the BID is one of the switch's MAC addresses; each switch has a pool of MAC addresses for this purpose, one for each instance of STP (one per VLAN).

Two BIDs are compared as follows: If (s,t) and (u,v) represent two BIDs (the first coordinate being the bridge priority and the second coordinate being the MAC address), (s,t) < (u,v) if and only if (i) s < u or (ii) s = u and t < v. Two BIDs cannot be equal because Catalyst switches are assigned unique pools of MAC addresses.

In this lab, the current root bridge is ALSwitch with a BID of (32768, 0002.4b21.36c0) because 0002.4b21.36c0 < 00-02-4b-59-40-00. (The MAC addresses determine the lowest BID because the default bridge priorities both equal 32768.) Notice the different MAC address formats used by the two switches. If you set the bridge priority to 1 on DLSwitch1 and the bridge priority to 100 on ALSwitch, DLSwitch1 has the smaller BID, because 1 < 100. Changing the priority to 1 on DLSwitch1 is sufficient, but you will change the priority to 100 on ALSwitch to illustrate the procedure for changing the priority on a 2900 XL.

Change the bridge priority to 1 on DLSwitch1:

```
DLSwitch1 (enable) set spantree priority 1
Spantree 1 bridge priority set to 1.
```

Immediately after issuing this command, check to see which switch is spanning tree's root bridge:

```
DLSwitch1 (enable) show spantree
VLAN 1
Spanning tree enabled
Spanning tree type          ieee

Designated Root             00-02-4b-59-40-00
Designated Root Priority    1
Designated Root Cost        0
Designated Root Port        1/0
Root Max Age   20 sec    Hello Time 2  sec   Forward Delay 15 sec

Bridge ID MAC ADDR          00-02-4b-59-40-00
Bridge ID Priority          1
Bridge Max Age 20 sec    Hello Time 2  sec   Forward Delay 15 sec
```

You see that the bridge priority is now 1 and the root bridge's MAC address now matches the BID MAC address of the Catalyst 4000 switch. This means that the 4000 switch is now the root bridge.

Just to make sure, examine the **show spanning-tree** command output on ALSwitch:

```
ALSwitch#show spanning-tree

Spanning tree 1 is executing the IEEE compatible Spanning Tree protocol
  Bridge Identifier has priority 32768, address 0002.4b21.36c0
  Configured hello time 2, max age 20, forward delay 15
  Current root has priority 1, address 0002.4b59.4000
  Root port is 25, cost of root path is 19
  Topology change flag not set, detected flag not set, changes 3
  Times:  hold 1, topology change 35, notification 2
          hello 2, max age 20, forward delay 15
  Timers: hello 0, topology change 0, notification 0
  Fast uplink switchover is enabled
```

Notice that it no longer tells you that you are the root bridge. It does give the MAC address and priority of the current root bridge.

In any case, you set the bridge priority to 100 on ALSwitch:

```
ALSwitch(config)#spanning-tree priority 100
```

Check again with the **show spanning-tree** command to make sure the priority has changed:

```
ALSwitch#show spanning-tree

Spanning tree 1 is executing the IEEE compatible Spanning Tree protocol
  Bridge Identifier has priority 100, address 0002.4b21.36c0
  Configured hello time 2, max age 20, forward delay 15
  Current root has priority 1, address 0002.4b59.4000
  Root port is 25, cost of root path is 19
  Topology change flag not set, detected flag not set, changes 3
  Times:  hold 1, topology change 35, notification 2
          hello 2, max age 20, forward delay 15
  Timers: hello 0, topology change 0, notification 0
  Fast uplink switchover is enabled
```

Notice that the bridge priority is now 100. You have successfully changed the root bridge to DLSwitch1.

Step 4

Now you want to force the uplink between port 2/34 and interface Fa0/12 to be the active link. First, you check the status of the current link.

Check the status on DLSwitch1:

```
DLSwitch1 (enable) show spantree
VLAN 1
Spanning tree enabled
Spanning tree type          ieee

Designated Root             00-02-4b-59-40-00
Designated Root Priority    1
Designated Root Cost        0
Designated Root Port        1/0
Root Max Age   20 sec    Hello Time 2  sec   Forward Delay 15 sec

Bridge ID MAC ADDR          00-02-4b-59-40-00
Bridge ID Priority          1
Bridge Max Age 20 sec    Hello Time 2  sec   Forward Delay 15 sec

Port                    Vlan Port-State   Cost  Priority Portfast   Channel_id
---------------------- ---- ------------- ----- -------- ---------- --- -------
 2/3                     1   forwarding    19         32 disabled   0
 2/34                    1   forwarding    19         32 disabled   0
```

Notice that both ports are forwarding. This is because DLSwitch1 is now the spanning-tree root. The backup link is blocked at the other (nonroot) end.

Check the status on ALSwitch:

```
ALSwitch#show spanning-tree interface fa0/1
Interface Fa0/1 (port 13) in Spanning tree 1 is FORWARDING
    Port path cost 19, Port priority 128
    Designated root has priority 1, address 0002.4b59.4000
    Designated bridge has priority 1, address 0002.4b59.4000
    Designated port is 67, path cost 0
    Timers: message age 2, forward delay 0, hold 0
    BPDU: sent 2301, received 447

ALSwitch#show spanning-tree interface fa0/12
Interface Fa0/12 (port 25) in Spanning tree 1 is BLOCKING
    Port path cost 19, Port priority 128
    Designated root has priority 1, address 0002.4b59.4000
    Designated bridge has priority 1, address 0002.4b59.4000
    Designated port is 98, path cost 0
    Timers: message age 2, forward delay 0, hold 0
    BPDU: sent 2295, received 466
```

As predicted, the higher-numbered port, interface Fa0/12, is the port that is blocking. Both links have port costs of 19.

1. How is this number determined? _____

Now configure the port path cost to force the uplink between port 2/34 and interface Fa0/12 to be the active uplink. As with the bridge priority, the lower the priority, the better when it comes to selecting which link will become the active link. You set the link that is currently blocked to a path cost of 1 and the other link to a path cost of 100 to make it the blocked link. Technically speaking, changing the path cost on the root bridge has no effect on the root path cost value carried by the BPDUs emanating from the root bridge (the Catalyst 4000 switch). However, the value is affected by setting the path cost on a candidate root port of a nonroot bridge, because the root path cost is incremented only upon the arrival of a BPDU at a nonroot bridge; in this case, the 2900 XL switch is a nonroot bridge.

On DLSwitch1:

```
DLSwitch1> (enable) set spantree portcost 2/34 1
Spantree port 2/34 path cost set to 1.
DLSwitch1> (enable) set spantree portcost 2/3 100
Spantree port 2/3 path cost set to 100.
```

Check on ALSwitch to see if anything changed.

2. Did anything change? _____

Now make changes on ALSwitch:

```
ALSwitch(config)#interface fa0/12
ALSwitch(config-if)#spanning-tree cost 1
ALSwitch(config-if)#interface fa0/1
ALSwitch(config-if)#spanning-tree cost 100
```

You might see a message like this:

```
01:42:27: %SPANTREE_FAST-6-PORT_FWD_UPLINK: Port FastEthernet0/12 in
  vlan 1 moved to Forwarding.
```

Now check your links again:

```
ALSwitch#show spanning-tree interface fa0/1
Interface Fa0/1 (port 13) in Spanning tree 1 is BLOCKING
    Port path cost 100, Port priority 128
    Designated root has priority 1, address 0002.4b59.4000
    Designated bridge has priority 1, address 0002.4b59.4000
    Designated port is 67, path cost 0
    Timers: message age 1, forward delay 0, hold 0
    BPDU: sent 2301, received 834

ALSwitch#show spanning-tree interface fa0/12
Interface Fa0/12 (port 25) in Spanning tree 1 is FORWARDING
    Port path cost 1, Port priority 128
    Designated root has priority 1, address 0002.4b59.4000
    Designated bridge has priority 1, address 0002.4b59.4000
    Designated port is 98, path cost 0
    Timers: message age 2, forward delay 0, hold 0
    BPDU: sent 2296, received 830
```

This shows that you were successful at forcing the backup uplink to become the active uplink.

Notice that the port path costs have changed. They are now set to 100 and 1.

This lab demonstrated how to change the spanning-tree topology using bridge priorities and port path costs.

Lab 5-3: Switched Port Analyzer

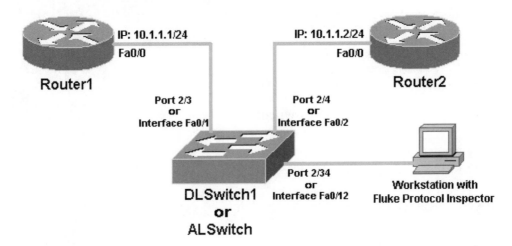

Objective

Use the Switched Port Analyzer (SPAN) feature to configure a port on your switch to monitor another port on the switch. This is used to capture data to a protocol analyzer.

Scenario

After converting your network from hubs to switches, you find it difficult to use your protocol analyzer to observe traffic between devices. Because switches filter traffic based on MAC address, you can no longer see traffic destined for a device on a particular port on any of the other ports. You need to set up a port on your switch as a monitor port or SPAN port. After you designate a port on your switch as a monitor port, you can copy input and output traffic from another port to your monitor port.

This lab contains commands for both the 2900 XL series and 4000 series Catalyst switches. You are encouraged to complete this lab twice—once for each platform.

Step 1

First, you need to configure two routers. These two routers will be used to create traffic between them. It is this traffic that you will capture with the Fluke Protocol Inspector.

The routers will not be configured with any routing protocol, just IP addresses on the Fast Ethernet interfaces of the 262*x* routers.

Router1:

```
Router(config)#hostname Router1
Router1(config)#interface fa0/0
Router1(config-if)#ip address 10.1.1.1 255.255.255.0
```

Router2:

```
Router(config)#hostname Router2
Router2(config)#interface fa0/0
Router2(config-if)#ip address 10.1.1.2 255.255.255.0
Router2(config-if)#line vty 0 4
Router2(config-line)#login
Router2(config-line)#password cisco
```

If you're using a Catalyst 4000 switch:

Plug Router1 into port 2/3.
Plug Router2 into port 2/4.

If you're using a Catalyst 2900 XL switch:

Plug Router1 into interface Fa0/1.
Plug Router2 into interface Fa0/2.

Make sure that the ports connecting to the routers are in the same VLAN.

Step 2

Test your router configuration by pinging Router2 from Router1. If you are unsuccessful, verify your router configuration.

Step 3

Take a workstation that has the Fluke Protocol Inspector software installed, and connect it to the following port.

If you're using a Catalyst 4000 switch:

Plug the protocol analyzer PC into port 2/34.

If you're using a Catalyst 2900 switch:

Plug the protocol analyzer PC into interface Fa0/12.

Make sure the PC is in the same VLAN as the routers. It is not necessary to configure an IP address on your PC because this PC will just be used to capture data with the analyzer. It will not send or receive any data of its own.

Step 4

You now need to configure the Ethernet switch to mirror traffic to the monitor/span port. You are interested only in capturing data from Router1's port.

The following commands configure a port as a monitor/span port. You will specify the port from which you want to "copy" frames and send them to the monitor/span port. Both frames transmitted and received will be copied to the monitor/span port.

If you're using a Catalyst 4000 switch:

```
DLSwitch1> (enable) set span 2/3 2/34
```

The first port specified is the port that the frames are copied from. The second port specified is the port to which the frames are copied. You have the option of copying many ports to the monitor/span port.

If you're using a Catalyst 2900 XL switch:

```
ALSwitch(config)#interface fa0/12
ALSwitch(config-if)#port monitor fa0/1
```

On the 2900 XL, you enter interface configuration mode on the port you use as the monitor port. Then, you use the **port monitor** command to specify which ports' frames are copied to this port.

Step 5

Verify your monitor/span port configuration.

If you're using a Catalyst 4000 switch:

Use the **show span** command to display which port is the destination (the port connected to the protocol analyzer) and which port is the source (the port you are monitoring):

```
DLSwitch1> (enable) show span

Destination      : Port 2/34
Admin Source     : Port 2/3
Oper Source      : Port 2/3
Direction        : transmit/receive
Incoming Packets: disabled
Learning         : enabled

---------------------------------------------
```

If you're using a Catalyst 2900 XL switch:

Use the **show port monitor** command to display which port is the monitor port (the port connected to the protocol analyzer) and which port is being monitored:

```
ALSwitch#show port monitor
Monitor Port            Port Being Monitored
--------------------    --------------------
FastEthernet0/12        FastEthernet0/1
```

Step 6

Start capturing data with your Fluke Protocol Inspector software.

From Router1, Telnet to Router2. Log in and issue several **show** commands to create traffic. Or, you can perform an extended ping to generate a large number of ICMP packets.

Check your protocol analyzer. You should see the traffic that was captured.

1. Can you capture more than one port to a monitor/span port? _____

2. Is it advisable to also capture the traffic from the switch port connected to Router2? Why?

_____

_____

_____

_____

_____

3. Can you think of any other precautions to take when using the monitor/span port?

_____

_____

_____

_____

Lab 5-4: Configuring Fast EtherChannel

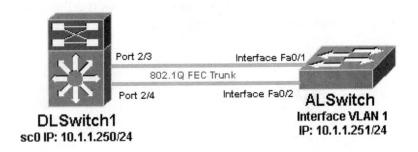

Objective

Achieve more bandwidth between switches by combining two 100 Mbps links to form a full-duplex 400 Mbps link.

Scenario

The uplink from your distribution layer switch to your access layer switch is congested due to the explosion of a new multicast application called SaturateBW. Your users served from ALSwitch are demanding more bandwidth. Rather than purchasing switches with Gigabit Ethernet ports, you have opted to use Fast EtherChannel, Cisco's method of scaling bandwidth for 100 Mbps Ethernet links.

You will add a second 100 Mbps Ethernet link between DLSwitch1 and ALSwitch and then configure them to operate as one logical link.

Step 1

Configure the passwords, name, and in-band management IP address for your Catalyst 4000 switch according to the diagram. If you like, you can use the same configuration you used in Lab 4-1 and skip this step:

```
Console> enable
Console> (enable) set system name DLSwitch1
System name set.
DLSwitch1> (enable)

DLSwitch1> (enable) set password
Enter old password:       (Because you do not currently have a password, press Enter.)
Enter new password:
Retype new password:
Password changed.

DLSwitch1> (enable) set enablepass
Enter old password:       (Because you do not currently have a password, press Enter.)
Enter new password:
Retype new password:
Password changed.

DLSwitch1> (enable) set interface sc0 10.1.1.250 255.255.255.0
DLSwitch1> (enable) set interface sc0 1
```

Step 2

Configure your 2900 XL switch name, passwords, and in-band management IP address according to the diagram. If you want to, you can use the same configuration you used in Lab 4-2 and skip this step:

```
Switch>enable
Switch#

Switch#configure terminal
Switch(config)#hostname ALSwitch
ALSwitch(config)#

ALSwitch(config)#enable password class
ALSwitch(config)#line console 0
ALSwitch(config-line)#password cisco
ALSwitch(config-line)#login
ALSwitch(config-line)#line vty 0 15
ALSwitch(config-line)#password cisco
ALSwitch(config-line)#login


ALSwitch(config)#interface vlan 1
ALSwitch(config-if)#ip address 10.1.1.251 255.255.255.0
```

Step 3

Connect an uplink cable from port 2/3 on DLSwitch1 to interface Fa0/1 on ALSwitch. Connect an uplink cable from port 2/4 on DLSwitch1 to interface Fa0/2 on ALSwitch. Remember to use crossover cables.

After you connect your cables and the switch detects the links, spanning tree goes into effect. Spanning tree disables one of the links. Confirm that the speed of these links is 100 Mbps and that the duplex setting for each link is full.

Step 4

You need to tell the switches to treat these two physical links as one logical link.

On DLSwitch1:

Instruct the switch to combine ports 2/3 and 2/4 into one logical channel:

```
DLSwitch1> (enable) set port channel 2/3-4 mode on
Port(s) 2/3-4 channel mode set to on.
```

On ALSwitch:

Instruct the switch to combine interfaces Fa0/1 and Fa0/2 into one logical channel:

```
ALSwitch(config)#interface fa0/1
ALSwitch(config-if)#port group 1 distribution destination
ALSwitch(config-if)#interface fa0/2
ALSwitch(config-if)#port group 1 distribution destination
```

The **distribution destination** keywords specify the forwarding method for the port group (channel group). The traffic is forwarded based on the frame's destination

MAC address. These keywords are optional. **distribution source** is the default setting.

The **channel-group** command replaces the **port group** command, which is used for Cisco IOS Software Releases prior to 12.1. In particular, the **port group** command is used on 2900 XL and 3500 XL switches, which do not support Release 12.1 or higher. To enable load distribution on Release 12.1 or higher, you must use an additional command in *global* configuration mode: **port-channel load-balance**.

If you are using a Catalyst 2950 with Cisco IOS Software Release 12.1(6)EA2 or later, or if you are using a Catalyst 3550 switch with Cisco IOS Software Release 12.1(4)EA1 or later, you can use the **interface range** command when creating EtherChannels to save some keystrokes.

In any case, you now have two 100 Mbps links bundled to provide an aggregate bandwidth of 400 Mbps (the full-duplex configuration allows for 200 Mbps in each direction).

Cisco's Fast EtherChannel (FEC) lets you combine eight 100 Mbps links for a 1600 Mbps (1.6 Gbps) full-duplex link. This allows scaling the bandwidth of links between 200 Mbps and 1.6 Gbps using FEC. The downside to this is that you would use up to eight Fast Ethernet ports on each switch to scale the link's bandwidth. With Gigabit Ethernet ports now readily available on 2950, 3500 XL, and 3550 switches, Fast EtherChannel is a relatively expensive way to scale link bandwidths (considering the cost of switch ports). On Catalyst 2950 and 3550 switches with sufficient Gigabit Ethernet port density, Gigabit EtherChannel (GEC) is available, providing bandwidth ranging from 2 Gbps to 16 Gbps. Also, with 10 Gigabit EtherChannel (10GEC) now available on Catalyst 6000 switches, EtherChannels comprised of 10 Gigabit Ethernet ports range in bandwidth from 20 Gbps to 160 Gbps (or .16 Terabits per second).

Step 5

Verify that the link is operational.

The Catalyst 4000 provides a command you can use to examine an EtherChannel's status:

```
DLSwitch1> (enable) show channel
Channel Id   Ports
----------   ----------------------------------------------
802          2/3-4
```

Test the new link's functionality by pinging DLSwitch1 from ALSwitch:

```
ALSwitch#ping 10.1.1.250

Type escape sequence to abort.
Sending 5, 100-byte ICMP Echos to 10.1.1.250, timeout is 2 seconds:
!!!!!
Success rate is 100 percent (5/5), round-trip min/avg/max = 5/9/11 ms
```

Use the **show port group** command on a 2900 XL switch to check the FEC's status from the perspective of the 2900 XL. The **show etherchannel** command replaces the **show port group** command for Cisco IOS Software Release 12.1 and higher.

Step 6

After the EtherChannel is established, you can configure trunking on it as well (using **set trunk** on the 4006 and **switchport mode trunk** on the 2900 XL). This allows you to trunk several VLANs over the combined links. Scaling trunk bandwidths is the most common use of EtherChannels. After an EtherChannel has formed, *configuring any port in the channel as a trunk applies the configuration to all ports in the channel*.

Lab 5-5: PortFast, UplinkFast, and BackboneFast

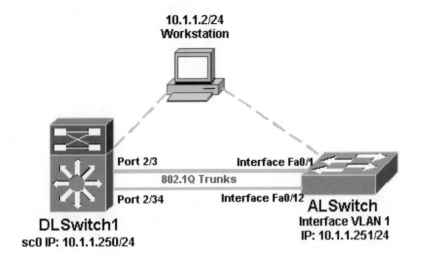

Objective

Use PortFast, UplinkFast, and BackboneFast to improve the time it takes for ports to transition through spanning-tree states.

Scenario

You just implemented a new redundant switched network. Your design is simple, yet elegant, and you think you have accounted for everything.

The first workday after your implementation, you start receiving calls from users, reporting that they can't log into their Windows domain. You discover their PCs are not getting an IP address from the DHCP server. You realize that when a workstation is powered on, it takes about 30 seconds for the port to become active. Because your workstations are the latest Pentium 4 machines, they boot up faster than the switch activates the port on the network. While the PC is requesting a DHCP address, the switch is still moving the port through spanning tree's Listening and Learning stages.

Also, you notice that when the active uplink between your two switches is broken, it takes the redundant link this same 30 seconds to complete the spanning-tree process before bringing up the backup (blocked) link. This results in a network outage for your users.

You will use the PortFast, UplinkFast, and BackboneFast commands to help spanning tree bring these convergence times down.

Step 1

Configure the passwords, name, and in-band management IP address for your Catalyst 4000 switch according to the diagram. If you like, you can use the same configuration you used in Lab 4-1 and skip this step:

```
Console> enable
Console> (enable) set system name DLSwitch1
System name set.
DLSwitch1> (enable)

DLSwitch1> (enable) set password
Enter old password:     (Because you do not currently have a password, press Enter.)
Enter new password:
Retype new password:
Password changed.

DLSwitch1> (enable) set enablepass
Enter old password:     (Because you do not currently have a password, press Enter.)
Enter new password:
Retype new password:
Password changed.

DLSwitch1(enable) set interface sc0 10.1.1.250 255.255.255.0
DLSwitch1(enable) set interface sc0 1
```

Step 2

Configure your 2900 XL switch name, passwords, and in-band management IP address according to the diagram. If you like, you can use the same configuration you used in Lab 4-2 and skip this step.

```
Switch>enable
Switch#
Switch#configure terminal
Switch(config)#hostname ALSwitch
ALSwitch(config)#

ALSwitch(config)#enable password class
ALSwitch(config)#line console 0
ALSwitch(config-line)#password cisco
ALSwitch(config-line)#login
ALSwitch(config-line)#line vty 0 15
ALSwitch(config-line)#password cisco
ALSwitch(config-line)#login


ALSwitch(config)#interface vlan 1
ALSwitch(config-if)#ip address 10.1.1.251 255.255.255.0
```

Step 3

Connect an uplink cable from port 2/3 on DLSwitch1 to interface Fa0/1 on ALSwitch. Connect an uplink cable from port 2/34 on DLSwitch1 to interface Fa0/12 on ALSwitch. Remember to use crossover cables.

You might notice that, no matter which order you install the uplinks in, the cable connecting port 2/3 to interface Fa0/1 becomes the active link.

Depending on which side of the link is blocking (the 2900 XL or the 4000 switch), you might have a hard time reading the lights. In Blocking state, the 2900 XL changes its light to a distinct yellow color. The 4000 switch, on the other hand, has very small port lights. If the 4000 switch side of the link is blocked, you might have a hard time viewing the lights. You can always use the **show spantree** command on the 4000 switch to view the port status:

```
DLSwitch> (enable) show spantree
VLAN 1
Spanning tree enabled
Spanning tree type          ieee

Designated Root             00-02-4b-21-36-c0
Designated Root Priority    32768
Designated Root Cost        19
Designated Root Port        2/3
Root Max Age    20 sec    Hello Time 2  sec   Forward Delay 15 sec

Bridge ID MAC ADDR          00-02-4b-59-40-00
Bridge ID Priority          32768
Bridge Max Age 20 sec     Hello Time 2  sec   Forward Delay 15 sec

Port                      Vlan Port-State     Cost  Priority Portfast   Channel_id
------------------------- ---- ------------- ----- -------- ---------- ----------
<output omitted>
 2/3                       1    forwarding      19        32 disabled   0
<output omitted>
 2/34                      1    blocking        19        32 disabled   0
```

Notice that port 2/34 is in Blocking state.

Step 4

Now let's observe spanning tree's default behavior. This is similar to what you did in Lab 5-1, "Spanning-Tree Protocol Default Behavior."

First, connect a workstation to any of the available ports on either switch. Power off your workstation and then power it back on. You will notice that as soon as the operating system initializes the NIC, the port turns yellow. The port is now active but is starting the spanning-tree process. Watch the PC boot up, and watch the color of the link light. You should observe that the PC makes it through most of the startup before the link turns green and active. This is where DHCP can miss its opportunity to get an IP address while spanning tree is transitioning through the Listening and Learning states.

You should observe that it takes about 30 seconds for a port connected to an end station to become active.

Now let's watch what happens when one of your uplinks changes its status.

Remove the active uplink cable (the port 2/3-to-interface Fa0/1 cable). Monitor the backup uplink ports. Watch the lights (to see if the 2900 XL indicates a yellow blocked port), or use the **show spantree** command on the 4000 switch (if the 4000 switch has the blocked end of the link).

You should observe that it takes about 30 seconds for the backup uplink ports to become active.

Now you will try to reduce the amount of time spanning tree needs to get these ports active.

Step 5

Configure PortFast.

You can use PortFast to force a port to skip the Listening and Learning spanning-tree states and go right to Forwarding state. It continues listening for a loop. If one exists, it places the port in Blocking state. You do run the risk of exposing your network to spanning-tree loops when using PortFast. Therefore, it is recommended that you use PortFast only on ports that you know will be used by end-user devices, and not other networking equipment, such as hubs, concentrators, bridges, and switches.

You must configure PortFast on each port individually. The Catalyst 4000 makes this easy, because you can specify a range of ports when enabling it. On the 2900 XL, you must enable PortFast on each port individually. If you are using a Catalyst 2950 with Cisco IOS Software Release 12.1(6)EA2 or later, or if you are using a Catalyst 3550 switch with Cisco IOS Software Release 12.1(4)EA1 or later, you can use the **interface range** command when enabling PortFast on interfaces to save some keystrokes.

Step 6

Configure PortFast on the Catalyst 4000:

```
DLSwitch1> (enable) set spantree portfast 2/4-2/33 enable

Warning: Spantree port fast start should only be enabled on ports
   connected to a single host.  Connecting hubs, concentrators, switches,
   bridges, etc. to a fast start port can cause temporary spanning tree
   loops.  Use with caution.

Spantree ports 2/4-33 fast start enabled.
```

You can set PortFast on all the remaining ports with just this one command. Notice that you skipped ports 2/3 and 2/34, because these are the ports you use as uplinks. Also notice the stern warning that is issued, informing you of the problems that PortFast can cause.

Step 7

Verify PortFast on the Catalyst 4000.

Remove your workstation from the switch, and plug it into any 10/100 port on the Catalyst 4000 L3 module.

You should see it go active right away. On the 4000 switch, you can refer to the **show spantree** command to verify the port state.

Step 8

Configure PortFast on the Catalyst 2900 XL:

```
ALSwitch(config)#interface fa0/2
ALSwitch(config-if)#spanning-tree portfast
ALSwitch(config-if)#interface fa0/3
ALSwitch(config-if)#spanning-tree portfast
ALSwitch(config-if)#interface fa0/4
ALSwitch(config-if)#spanning-tree portfast
ALSwitch(config-if)#interface fa0/5
ALSwitch(config-if)#spanning-tree portfast
ALSwitch(config-if)#interface fa0/6
ALSwitch(config-if)#spanning-tree portfast
ALSwitch(config-if)#interface fa0/7
ALSwitch(config-if)#spanning-tree portfast
ALSwitch(config-if)#interface fa0/8
ALSwitch(config-if)#spanning-tree portfast
ALSwitch(config-if)#interface fa0/9
ALSwitch(config-if)#spanning-tree portfast
ALSwitch(config-if)#interface fa0/10
ALSwitch(config-if)#spanning-tree portfast
ALSwitch(config-if)#interface fa0/11
ALSwitch(config-if)#spanning-tree portfast
```

Remember not to configure PortFast on interfaces Fa0/1 and Fa0/12 because they are being used as uplinks.

Step 9

Verify PortFast on the Catalyst 2900 XL.

Disconnect your workstation from the switch, and plug it into any available port on the 2900 XL switch.

You should see it go active right away. With the 2900 XL, you can see the lights go green immediately, without the "Learning/Listening" period indicated by the yellow light.

Use the **show spanning-tree** command to check what state each link is in:

```
ALSwitch#show spanning-tree

Spanning tree 1 is executing the IEEE compatible Spanning Tree protocol
  Bridge Identifier has priority 49152, address 0002.4b21.36c0
  Configured hello time 2, max age 20, forward delay 15
  We are the root of the spanning tree
```

```
     Topology change flag not set, detected flag not set, changes 5
     Times:  hold 1, topology change 35, notification 2
             hello 2, max age 20, forward delay 15
     Timers: hello 0, topology change 0, notification 0
     Fast uplink switchover is enabled

 Interface Fa0/1 (port 13) in Spanning tree 1 is FORWARDING
    Port path cost 3019, Port priority 128
    Designated root has priority 49152, address 0002.4b21.36c0
    Designated bridge has priority 49152, address 0002.4b21.36c0
    Designated port is 13, path cost 0
    Timers: message age 0, forward delay 0, hold 0
    BPDU: sent 2089, received 45

 Interface Fa0/12 (port 25) in Spanning tree 1 is FORWARDING
    Port path cost 3019, Port priority 128
    Designated root has priority 49152, address 0002.4b21.36c0
    Designated bridge has priority 49152, address 0002.4b21.36c0
    Designated port is 25, path cost 0
    Timers: message age 0, forward delay 0, hold 0
    BPDU: sent 3222, received 42
```

Step 10

Configure UplinkFast.

You want to speed up the process of switching over from the active uplink to the blocked uplink in case the active uplink fails. UplinkFast was developed to facilitate fast STP convergence. UplinkFast is a Catalyst feature that accelerates the choice of a new root port when a link or switch fails.

The **uplinkfast** command is a command that affects all VLANs and ports. There is no way to issue **uplinkfast** on just one port or VLAN.

On the Catalyst 4000, use the following:

```
DLSwitch1> (enable) set spantree uplinkfast enable
VLANs 1-1005 bridge priority set to 49152.
The port cost and portvlancost of all ports set to above 3000.
Station update rate set to 15 packets/100ms.
uplinkfast all-protocols field set to off.
uplinkfast enabled for bridge.
```

On ALSwitch (Catalyst 2900 XL), use the following:

```
ALSwitch(config)#spanning-tree uplinkfast
```

Step 11

Verify UplinkFast.

Remove the active uplink cable. Watch the lights and/or the **show spantree** output on DLSwitch1. You should see the blocked uplink come active much quicker than the 30 seconds it took without the **uplinkfast** command.

1. How long did it take the blocked link to become active? _____

Step 12

Configure BackboneFast.

BackboneFast modifies how the switch evaluates spanning-tree rules when a switch receives inferior BPDUs from its designated bridge on its root port or blocked ports (in the event of an indirect link failure, which UplinkFast cannot address). This phenomenon occurs when the designated bridge loses its connection to the root bridge. BPDUs are received from a switch that identifies itself as both the root bridge and the designated bridge. Under normal spanning-tree rules, these BPDUs are ignored for the maximum aging time. BackboneFast modifies these rules and tells the switch to ignore these timers. If an uplink changes status and there is another backup link, BackboneFast causes the switch to bypass the maxage timer and move immediately to the Listening/Learning states (saving 20 seconds). If the switch determines that there is no longer another path to the root bridge, it immediately expires the maximum aging timer and removes that link.

This results in much faster convergence when you have multiple links in your switched network.

BackboneFast is supported on the Catalyst 4000 series switches, but not the 2900 XL switch. It is also supported on Catalyst 2950 and 3550 switches with Cisco IOS Software Release 12.1 and higher. Here is how you configure BackboneFast on a Catalyst 4000 switch:

```
DLSwitch1> (enable) set spantree backbonefast enable
Backbonefast enabled for all VLANs.
```

Step 13

Verify Backbone Fast operation using the following:

```
DLSwitch1> (enable) show spantree backbonefast
Backbonefast is enabled.
```

This lab demonstrated the configuration of spanning-tree PortFast, UplinkFast, and BackboneFast. Because not all your devices support BackboneFast (and because it needs to be configured on all switches in a spanning tree), this lab did not demonstrate the mechanism of BackboneFast.

Lab 6-1: Router-on-a-Stick

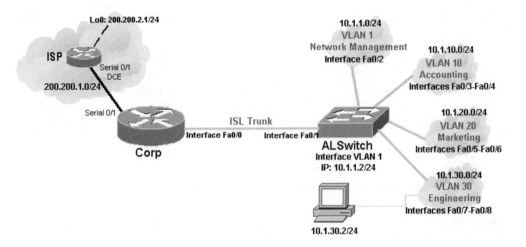

Objective

Configure an external router to route inter-VLAN traffic (router-on-a-stick).

Scenario

Network loads and management issues require you to segment your network from a single broadcast domain into four functional areas. You decide to implement VLANs throughout your Cisco 2900 XL switched network and call them "Accounting," "Marketing," and "Engineering" for the users and "default" for the network management VLAN. After itemizing your subnet ranges and VTP parameters, your next step is to implement inter-VLAN routing using a Cisco 2600 series router. Inter-VLAN routing allows clients and servers on the various VLANs to exchange data. Your 2600 series WAN router provides a 56 Kbps WAN connection to your ISP and a 100 Mbps Ethernet connection to a switch in your private network. Because you have only a single Ethernet connection between the router and the switch, the "router-on-a-stick" solution is used to support inter-VLAN routing.

Design

Catalyst 2900 XL VTP configuration:

VTP Domain	VTP Mode
Corp	Server

VLAN configuration:

VLAN ID	VLAN Name	VLAN Subnet	VLAN Gateway	Switch Ports
1	default	10.1.1.0/24	10.1.1.1	2
10	Accounting	10.1.10.0/24	10.1.10.1	3 and 4
20	Marketing	10.1.20.0/24	10.1.20.1	5 and 6
30	Engineering	10.1.30.0/24	10.1.30.1	7 and 8
Trunk	—	—	—	1, ISL full-duplex

Cisco 2600 interface configuration:

Interface	IP Address	VLAN	NAT
FastEthernet 0/0.1	10.1.1.1/24	1 "native"	Inside
FastEthernet 0/0.10	10.1.10.1/24	10	Inside
FastEthernet 0/0.20	10.1.20.1/24	20	Inside
FastEthernet 0/0.30	10.1.30.1/24	30	Inside
Serial0/1	200.200.1.2/24	—	Outside

Notes

_____
_____
_____
_____
_____
_____
_____
_____
_____
_____
_____
_____
_____
_____

Step 1

Cable the lab as shown in the diagram.

Step 2

The first router to be configured is the ISP router. Access the router through the console port and enter privileged mode. Clear the NVRAM and reload. The ISP router is not a core part of the lab but a supplemental device for real-world illustration.

Step 3

Configure the ISP router with the following information:

a. Configure the host name, ISP, on the 2600 router:

```
Router(config)#hostname ISP
```

b. Configure the loopback 0 interface to represent a remote network:

```
ISP(config)#interface Loopback0
ISP(config-if)#ip address 200.200.2.1 255.255.255.0
```

Note: Verify using **show run**.

c. Configure the serial 0/1 interface on the ISP router that connects to the Corp router:

```
ISP(config)#interface Serial0/1
ISP(config-if)#ip address 200.200.1.1 255.255.255.0
ISP(config-if)#clock rate 56000
ISP(config-if)#no shutdown
```

Note: Verify using **show run**.

d. Configure a default route on ISP to "bounce" back traffic to the Corp network for testing:

```
ISP(config)#ip route 0.0.0.0 0.0.0.0 200.200.1.2
```

Note: Verify using **show run**.

Step 4

Show a summary of the interface configurations to verify configured IP addresses:

```
ISP#show ip interface brief
```

1. What is the status of the loopback 0 interface?

_____

2. What is the status of the serial 0/1 interface?

_____

Note: The serial interface should be in a DOWN state, because the Corp router is not yet configured. The loopback 0 interface should always be in an UP state by default.

Step 5

If necessary, erase the configuration on the Corp router and reload the router. Configure the Corp router with the following information:

a. Configure the host name, Corp, on the 2600 router:

```
Router(config)#hostname Corp
```

b. The router needs to talk to the switch using a trunking protocol. There are two primary trunking protocols: ISL and 802.1Q. In this lab, the FastEthernet connection will use ISL trunking. First you configure the main interface. Note that no IP address is necessary, but you specify that the connection between the router and the switch is full duplex. Do not forget to enable the interface with the **no shutdown** command:

```
Corp(config)#interface FastEthernet0/0
Corp(config-if)#full-duplex
Corp(config-if)#no shutdown
```

Note: Verify using **show run**.

c. We now address the main focus of this lab: the inter-VLAN connection to the switch. The configuration is fairly simple in that each VLAN requires its own subinterface; that includes the encapsulation and VLAN ID along with the IP address for the gateway interface for all hosts on that VLAN. You will also add additional functional information, including NAT and a description for documentation:

VLAN 1 Interface
```
Corp(config)#interface FastEthernet0/0.1
Corp(config-subif)#description Management VLAN 1
Corp(config-subif)#encapsulation isl 1
Corp(config-subif)#ip address 10.1.1.1 255.255.255.0
Corp(config-subif)#ip nat inside
```

VLAN 10 Interface
```
Corp(config)#interface FastEthernet0/0.10
Corp(config-subif)#description Accounting VLAN 10
Corp(config-subif)#encapsulation isl 10
Corp(config-subif)#ip address 10.1.10.1 255.255.255.0
Corp(config-subif)#ip nat inside
```

VLAN 20 Interface
```
Corp(config)#interface FastEthernet0/0.20
Corp(config-subif)#description Marketing VLAN 20
Corp(config-subif)#encapsulation isl 20
Corp(config-subif)#ip address 10.1.20.1 255.255.255.0
Corp(config-subif)#ip nat inside
```

VLAN 30 Interface
```
Corp(config)#interface FastEthernet0/0.30
Corp(config-subif)#description Engineering VLAN 30
Corp(config-subif)#encapsulation isl 30
Corp(config-subif)#ip address 10.1.30.1 255.255.255.0
Corp(config-subif)#ip nat inside
```

Note: Verify using **show run**.

Step 6

Show a summary of the interface configuration to verify configured IP subinterface addresses:

```
Corp#show ip interface brief
```

3. Are all the interfaces in the UP state?

_____

Step 7

Next, you configure the serial connection to the ISP:

```
Corp(config)#interface Serial0/1
Corp(config-if)#ip address 200.200.1.2 255.255.255.0
Corp(config-if)#ip nat outside
Corp(config-if)#no shutdown
Corp(config-if)#end
```

Note: Verify using **show run**.

Step 8

It's time to verify your Internet connection. Ping the ISP interface and the ISP's loopback 0 interface. Both should function before you continue with this exercise. If there is a problem, verify your cable connections and IP address assignments.

```
Corp#ping 200.200.1.2
```

```
Corp#ping 200.200.1.1
```

```
Corp#ping 200.200.2.1
```

4. Were all the pings successful? _____

Step 9

For the Corp router, you configure the NAT information and the gateway of last resort to the ISP. Instead of creating a NAT pool, you simply use the serial interface already configured:

```
Corp(config)#ip nat inside source list 1 interface Serial0/1 overload
Corp(config)#access-list 1 permit any
Corp(config)#ip route 0.0.0.0 0.0.0.0 200.200.1.1
```

Note: Verify using **show run**.

Step 10

If necessary, erase the ALSwitch configuration, delete the vlan.dat file, and reload the switch. Configure the ALSwitch switch with the following information:

a. Configure the host name, ALSwitch, on the 2900 XL switch:

```
Switch(config)#hostname ALSwitch
```

b. Configure the secret password **cisco** on the 2900 XL switch:

```
ALSwitch(config)#enable secret cisco
```

Note: Verify using **show run**.

c. Configure the switch's IP address, default gateway, and vty parameters for network management. The switch will be set to IP address 10.1.1.2 because the router has a gateway address already set to 10.1.1.1. A default gateway is configured to allow for packets sourced from the switch to be routed successfully:

```
ALSwitch(config)#interface VLAN1
ALSwitch(config-if)#ip address 10.1.1.2 255.255.255.0
ALSwitch(config-if)#exit

ALSwitch(config)#ip default-gateway 10.1.1.1

ALSwitch(config)#line vty 0 4
ALSwitch(config-line)#password cisco
ALSwitch(config-line)#login
ALSwitch(config-line)#end
```

Note: Verify using **show run**.

Step 11

Configure the VLAN database on the 2900 XL.

a. Start by displaying the VLANs that are currently on the switch:

```
ALSwitch#show vlan
```

5. What VLAN IDs appear? _____

b. VLAN IDs 1, 1002, 1003, 1004, and 1005 are the defaults. Enter VLAN configuration mode:

```
ALSwitch#vlan database
```

6. Does your new command prompt look like this: ALSwitch(vlan)#?

_____

c. Set the VTP information. If it is already set, this command simply verifies:

```
ALSwitch(vlan)#vtp domain Corp
ALSwitch(vlan)#vtp server
```

d. Add the corporate VLANs to the database:

```
ALSwitch(vlan)#vlan 10 name Accounting
ALSwitch(vlan)#vlan 20 name Marketing
ALSwitch(vlan)#vlan 30 name Engineering
```

e. Verify the VLAN information with the following command:

```
ALSwitch(vlan)#show (there are no parameters)
```

7. What VLANs are displayed?

_____

8. What is the common MTU?

_____

9. What are the FDDI VLAN IDs for each ISL ID?

_____

f. Verify the VLAN statistics information. Issue the following commands and then fill in the blanks:

```
ALSwitch(vlan)#exit
ALSwitch1#show vtp stat
```

Fill in the following:

VTP version: _____

Configuration revision: _____

Maximum VLANs supported locally: _____

Number of existing VLANs: _____

VTP operating mode: _____

VTP domain name: _____

VTP pruning mode: _____

VTP V2 mode: _____

VTP traps generation: _____

Step 12

Configure the switch for trunking, and assign VLANs to identified interfaces according to the VLAN configuration table at the beginning of this lab.

a. Set the interface connected to the router to trunk with the router. You might recall that the router is already set to trunk with the VLAN subinterfaces. The default encapsulation is ISL, so the command **switchport trunk encapsulation isl** is unnecessary:

```
ALSwitch(config)#interface FastEthernet0/1
ALSwitch(config-if)#switchport mode trunk
```

Note: Verify using **show run**.

b. To verify that the trunking is working properly, look at the CDP information:

```
ALSwitch#show cdp neighbor detail
```

10. What is the neighbor's IP address? _____

    c. Assign the correct VLANs to each port, and additionally configure the ports with PortFast so that you don't have to wait for spanning tree to iterate through the Listening and Learning states:

```
ALSwitch(config)#interface FastEthernet0/2
ALSwitch(config-if)#switchport access vlan 1
ALSwitch(config-if)#spanning-tree portfast

ALSwitch(config)#interface FastEthernet0/3
ALSwitch(config-if)#switchport access vlan 10
ALSwitch(config-if)#spanning-tree portfast

ALSwitch(config)#interface FastEthernet0/4
ALSwitch(config-if)#switchport access vlan 10
ALSwitch(config-if)#spanning-tree portfast

ALSwitch(config)#interface FastEthernet0/5
ALSwitch(config-if)#switchport access vlan 20
ALSwitch(config-if)#spanning-tree portfast

ALSwitch(config)#interface FastEthernet0/6
ALSwitch(config-if)#switchport access vlan 20
ALSwitch(config-if)#spanning-tree portfast

ALSwitch(config)#interface FastEthernet0/7
ALSwitch(config-if)#switchport access vlan 30
ALSwitch(config-if)#spanning-tree portfast

ALSwitch(config)#interface FastEthernet0/8
ALSwitch(config-if)#switchport access vlan 30
ALSwitch(config-if)#spanning-tree portfast
```

    Note: Verify using **show run**.

Step 13

The configuration is complete. Now verify the configuration and host access:

    a. Ensure that your workstation is connected to a port on the switch that is set to VLAN 30 (Engineering). This should be port 7 or 8. The workstation IP address should be set to 10.1.30.2/24 with a gateway of 10.1.30.1.

    b. From a command prompt on the workstation, ping the following addresses:

```
Inter-VLAN Gateway → C:\>ping 10.1.30.1
ALSwitch → C:\>ping 10.1.1.2
Corp Router Public Interface → C:\>ping 200.200.1.2
ISP Router → C:\>ping 200.200.1.1
ISP loopback → C:\>ping 200.200.2.1
```

11. Did any of the pings fail? _____

Step 14

Finally, you want to be able to remotely manage the switch. Remember that VLAN 1 is the default management VLAN and that all devices have an IP address on VLAN 1. Your switch, as you recall, is set to IP address 10.1.1.2, and the router gateway for VLAN 1 is 10.1.1.1.

From the DOS command prompt on your workstation, Telnet to the switch. Log on using the password **cisco**.

```
C:\>telnet 10.1.1.2
```

This lab demonstrated how to configure router-on-a-stick with a 2900 XL switch and a 2600 series router.

Lab 6-2: Configuring the L3 Services Module on a Catalyst 4006 Switch

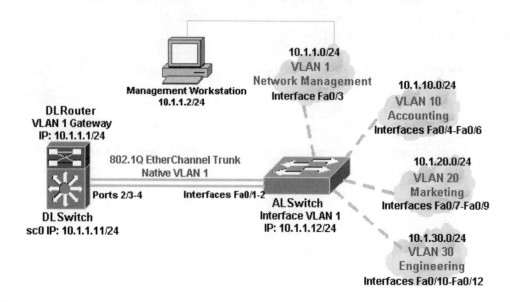

Objective

Configure the L3 Services Module on a Catalyst 4006 switch.

Scenario

Your network switching equipment currently includes a Catalyst 4006 core switch and a 2900 XL access switch. You need to segment your network from a single broadcast domain into four functional areas for better network management. You decide to implement VLANs throughout your Cisco switched network and call them "Accounting," "Marketing," and "Engineering" for the users and "default" for the native VLAN used for network management. After deciding on your subnet ranges and VTP information, as shown in the following tables, your next step is to implement inter-VLAN routing. Inter-VLAN routing allows individual hosts and servers on your VLANs to exchange information. To facilitate this functionality, you choose to install a Layer 3 Services Module for the 4006 and establish VLAN trunking to the 2900 XL switch over a Fast EtherChannel link.

Design

VTP configuration information:

Switch	VTP Domain	VTP Mode
DLSwitch	Corp	Server
ALSwitch	Corp	Client

VLAN configuration information:

VLAN ID	VLAN Name	VLAN Subnet	VLAN Gateway
1	default	10.1.1.0/24	10.1.1.1
10	Accounting	10.1.10.0/24	10.1.10.1
20	Marketing	10.1.20.0/24	10.1.20.1
30	Engineering	10.1.30.0/24	10.1.30.1

Catalyst 4006 and 2900 XL VLAN port/interface assignments:

Switch	VLAN 1	VLAN 10	VLAN 20	VLAN 30	Trunk
DLSwitch	5 to 18	19 to 24	25 to 30	31 to 34	3 and 4
ALSwitch	3	4 to 6	7 to 9	10 to 12	1 and 2

Catalyst 4006 DLRouter interface configuration information:

Interface	IP Address	VLAN
PortChannel 1.1	10.1.1.1/24	1 (native)
PortChannel 1.10	10.1.10.1/24	10
PortChannel 1.20	10.1.20.1/24	20
PortChannel 1.30	10.1.30.1/24	30

Notes

Lab Tasks

Step 1

Cable the lab as shown in the diagram.

Step 2

The first device to be configured is the distribution layer switch DLSwitch. Access the switch through the console port and enter privileged mode. Clear your NVRAM and reload.

```
Switch (enable) clear config all
Switch (enable) reset
```

1. About how long did it take to reboot the switch?

Step 3

Configure DLSwitch with the following information:

    a.   Configure the system name DLSwitch on the 4006 switch:

```
Console> (enable) set system name DLSwitch
```

    Note: Verify using **show config**.

    b.   Configure VTP information on the 4006 switch. The core switch (here we have a collapsed core) should always be set as a VTP server. You might recall that pruning can be configured only on VTP servers. This issue sometimes leads to individuals setting all network switches to VTP servers, but that is not recommended, because pruning is mostly needed at the distribution layer, not the access layer.

```
DLSwitch> (enable) set vtp domain Corp
DLSwitch> (enable) set vtp mode server
```

    Note: Verify using **show vtp domain**.

2. What VTP version is running?

---

    c.   Create corporate VLANs. You might find it easier to configure VLANs on CatOS switches than on IOS-based switches. You create and name the VLANs first and assign ports later. When the connection is established to the 2900 XL, the 4006 synchronizes with the 2900 XL database so that the assigned ports gain access:

```
DLSwitch> (enable) set vlan 1 name default
DLSwitch> (enable) set vlan 10 name Accounting
DLSwitch> (enable) set vlan 20 name Marketing
DLSwitch> (enable) set vlan 30 name Engineering
```

    Note: Verify using **show vlan**.

3. What accounts for the additional VLANs beyond 1, 10, 20, 30?

---

d. Set the switch IP address information and gateway. Again, this is for management; it is not required for switch functionality. It is assumed that you'll want to Telnet to the switch.

```
DLSwitch> (enable) set interface sc0 up
DLSwitch> (enable) set interface sc0 1 10.1.1.11/255.255.255.0
10.1.1.255
DLSwitch> (enable) set ip route 0.0.0.0/0.0.0.0 10.1.1.1
```

Note: Verify using **show config**.

e. (Optional) Set the port channel admin groups. Otherwise, the switch assigns these automatically. The switch uses the port channel admin groups for internal purposes.

```
DLSwitch> (enable) set port channel 2/1-2 156
DLSwitch> (enable) set port channel 2/3-4 157
```

Note: Verify using **show config**.

f. Assign VLAN memberships to ports. If you use the **show vlan** command, you see that all ports default to VLAN 1. You can easily set blocks of ports to specific VLANs, unlike the 2900 XL switches, where you have to configure VLANs one interface at a time.

```
DLSwitch> (enable) set vlan 10 2/19-24
DLSwitch> (enable) set vlan 20 2/25-30
DLSwitch> (enable) set vlan 30 2/31-34
```

Note: Verify using **show vlan**.

4. What is the command to delete a VLAN?

---

g. Establish VLAN trunking. These commands let you establish trunking—first between the 4006 virtual switch ports 2/1-2 and the L3 Services Module, and second between the 4006 external switch ports 2/3-4 and the 2900 XL.

```
DLSwitch> (enable) set trunk 2/1 nonegotiate dot1q 1-1005
DLSwitch> (enable) set trunk 2/2 nonegotiate dot1q 1-1005
DLSwitch> (enable) set trunk 2/3 nonegotiate dot1q 1-1005
DLSwitch> (enable) set trunk 2/4 nonegotiate dot1q 1-1005
```

Note: Verify using **show config**.

5. Why would **show trunk** not show the trunking you just set?

---

h. Establish EtherChannels on the trunking interfaces. You are running a Gigabit EtherChannel (GEC) to the L3 module on ports 2/1-2 and a Fast EtherChannel (FEC) on ports 3-4 to the 2900 XL:

```
DLSwitch> (enable) set port channel 2/1-2 mode on
DLSwitch> (enable) set port channel 2/3-4 mode on
```

Note: Verify using **show channel**.

i. Set the switch passwords. You use **cisco** throughout this lab for all passwords:

```
DLSwitch> (enable) set enablepass <enter>
```

You are prompted to enter and confirm the password:

```
DLSwitch> (enable) set password <enter>
```

You are prompted to enter and confirm the password.

j. Verify a complete configuration using **show config**.

Step 4

The next device to be configured is the access layer switch, ALSwitch. Access the switch through the console port, and enter privileged mode. Clear the NVRAM and reload. Deleting the vlan.dat file prevents the inadvertent propagation of unwanted VLAN information throughout the VTP domain:

```
Switch#delete vlan.dat
Switch#erase start
Switch#reload
```

Note: If you're asked whether you want to save system information, select **No**.

Step 5

Configure the ALSwitch switch with the following information:

a. Configure VTP information. Note that ALSwitch learns the VTP domain name Corp from the 4006 switch, but you include the command here for completion:

```
Switch#vlan database
Switch(vlan)#vtp client
Switch(vlan)#vtp domain Corp
Switch(vlan)#exit
```

b. Verify VTP information. This lets you check the information you just entered. Throughout this lab, you'll need to enter and then verify, simply because you cannot officially test the network until most of the components are configured:

```
Switch#show vtp stat
```

Complete the following:

VTP version: _____
Configuration revision: _____
Maximum VLANs supported locally: _____
Number of existing VLANs: _____
VTP operating mode: _____
VTP domain name: _____
VTP pruning mode: _____
VTP V2 mode: _____
VTP traps generation: _____

c. Configure the host name, ALSwitch, on the 2900 XL switch:

```
Switch(config)#hostname ALSwitch
```

Note: Verify using **show run**.

d. Configure the privileged-mode password. These passwords are necessary to establish Telnet sessions. All passwords for this lab are **cisco**:

```
ALSwitch(config)#enable password cisco
```

Note: Verify using **show run**.

e. Configure a Fast EtherChannel port group, and configure trunking. The backbone is 1 Gbps, and the 2900 XL switch offers 100 Mbps to each workstation. Therefore, it makes sense to establish all your uplinks at a minimum of 200 Mbps to the main distribution switch. You use the first two switch ports for this task. On a 2900XL or 3500XL switch, Fast EtherChannels are called *port groups*. The **port group** command is used on 2900 XL and 3500 XL switches, which do not support Release 12.1 or higher. The **channel-group** command replaces the **port group** command on IOS-based switches supporting IOS 12.1 or higher. CatOS switches call bundles *channel groups*. Here, you set the group to encompass two ports and the trunking protocol to be 802.1Q:

```
ALSwitch(config)#interface FastEthernet0/1
ALSwitch(config-if)#port group 1
ALSwitch(config-if)#switchport trunk encapsulation dot1q
ALSwitch(config-if)#switchport mode trunk

ALSwitch(config)#interface FastEthernet0/2
ALSwitch(config-if)#port group 1
ALSwitch(config-if)#switchport trunk encapsulation dot1q
ALSwitch(config-if)#switchport mode trunk
```

Note: Verify using **show run**.

6. What is the default encapsulation for trunking?

---

f. Configure port VLAN memberships and spanning tree PortFast. Here you configure the device connection parameters. At the least, you assign the VLANs and set PortFast for each end station-connected interface. PortFast should be set on for all non-switch-to-switch connections. This lab was created with a 12-port 2900 XL, but you might have more ports:

```
ALSwitch(config)#interface FastEthernet0/3
ALSwitch(config-if)#switchport access vlan 1
ALSwitch(config-if)#spanning-tree portfast

ALSwitch(config)#interface FastEthernet0/4
ALSwitch(config-if)#switchport access vlan 10
ALSwitch(config-if)#spanning-tree portfast

ALSwitch(config)#interface FastEthernet0/5
ALSwitch(config-if)#switchport access vlan 10
ALSwitch(config-if)#spanning-tree portfast

ALSwitch(config)#interface FastEthernet0/6
ALSwitch(config-if)#switchport access vlan 10
ALSwitch(config-if)#spanning-tree portfast

ALSwitch(config)#interface FastEthernet0/7
ALSwitch(config-if)#switchport access vlan 20
ALSwitch(config-if)#spanning-tree portfast

ALSwitch(config)#interface FastEthernet0/8
ALSwitch(config-if)#switchport access vlan 20
ALSwitch(config-if)#spanning-tree portfast

ALSwitch(config)#interface FastEthernet0/9
ALSwitch(config-if)#switchport access vlan 20
ALSwitch(config-if)#spanning-tree portfast

ALSwitch(config)#interface FastEthernet0/10
ALSwitch(config-if)#switchport access vlan 30
ALSwitch(config-if)#spanning-tree portfast

ALSwitch(config)#interface FastEthernet0/11
ALSwitch(config-if)#switchport access vlan 30
ALSwitch(config-if)#spanning-tree portfast

ALSwitch(config)#interface FastEthernet0/12
ALSwitch(config-if)#switchport access vlan 30
ALSwitch(config-if)#spanning-tree portfast
```

Note: Verify using **show run**.

7. What is the VLAN for all ports by default?

---

g. Configure the VLAN 1 management interface IP address and default gateway for the switch. This is required only for management; it will not affect the device's functionality. This interface is up by default, so **no shutdown** should not be necessary, but you should check anyway. The **show ip interface brief** command helps with that:

```
ALSwitch(config)#ip default-gateway 10.1.1.1

ALSwitch(config)#interface VLAN1
ALSwitch(config-if)#ip address 10.1.1.12 255.255.255.0
```

Note: Verify using **show run**.

h. Configure the vty line password. This is required if you want to Telnet to the switch:

```
ALSwitch(config)#line vty 0 4
ALSwitch(config-line)#password cisco
ALSwitch(config-line)#login
```

i. Verify the complete configuration using **show run**. Go ahead and compare it to the configuration at the end of the lab. Don't worry about little differences because the switch places a number of its own configuration commands.

Step 6

The next device to be configured is the distribution layer router, DLRouter. Access the router through the DLSwitch console port (using the **session** command), and enter privileged mode on the router. Clear your NVRAM and reload:

```
DLSwitch> (enable) session 2
Router#clear start
Router#reload
```

Note: If you're asked whether you want to save system information, select **No**.

After the card reset, go back into the router:

```
DLSwitch> (enable) session 2
```

8. How do you return from the router to the switch?

Step 7

Configure DLRouter with the following information:

a. Configure the host name, DLRouter, on the 4006 L3 module:

```
Router(config)#hostname DLRouter
```

Note: Verify using **show run**.

b. Configure the privileged-mode password. This is required for Telnet access:

```
DLRouter(config)#enable password cisco
```

Note: Verify using **show run**.

c. Configure the VLAN interface addressing and trunking information. Notice that you put the management VLAN on the main interface and the other VLANs on subinterfaces. This allows communication throughout the network within VLAN 1 for the purposes of network management (you can think of this as out-of-band management). However, communication between VLAN 1 and the other VLANs is impossible; only communication between VLANs other than 1 is possible:

```
DLRouter (config)#interface Port-channel1
DLRouter (config-if)#ip address 10.1.1.1 255.255.255.0
DLRouter (config-if)#no shutdown

DLRouter (config)#interface Port-channel1.10
DLRouter (config-if)#encapsulation dot1Q 10
DLRouter (config-if)#ip address 10.1.10.1 255.255.255.0

DLRouter (config)#interface Port-channel1.20
DLRouter (config-if)#encapsulation dot1Q 20
DLRouter (config-if)#ip address 10.1.20.1 255.255.255.0

DLRouter (config)#interface Port-channel1.30
DLRouter (config-if)#encapsulation dot1Q 30
DLRouter (config-if)#ip address 10.1.30.1 255.255.255.0
```

Note: Verify using **show run**.

9. What would happen if you tried to use ISL trunking?

_____

d. Assign the gigabit interfaces to the port channel interface. This completes the GEC configuration:

```
DLRouter(config)#interface GigabitEthernet3
DLRouter(config-if)#channel-group 1

DLRouter(config)#interface GigabitEthernet4
DLRouter(config-if)#channel-group 1
```

Note: Verify using **show run**.

e. Configure your corporate routing protocol. This is actually not required in this topology because all routed interfaces are directly connected to DLRouter interfaces. Setting it to EIGRP ensures that only Cisco devices can read the L3 routing table, if necessary. You configure the entire 10.0.0.0/8 network:

```
DLRouter(config)#router eigrp 1
DLRouter(config-router)#network 10.0.0.0
```

Note: Verify using **show run**.

10. Can any routing protocol effectively be used here?

---

      f. Configure your Telnet virtual terminal password information:

```
DLRouter(config)#line vty 0 4
DLRouter(config-line)#password cisco
DLRouter(config-line)#login
```

        Note: Verify using **show run**.

      g. Verify the complete configuration using **show run**.

Step 8

From DLRouter, verify your connection to DLSwitch through the port channel:

```
DLRouter#show cdp neighbors
```

11. What is the name of the neighboring device?

Check the status of the interfaces:

```
DLRouter#show ip interface brief
```

12. Why would the GigabitEthernet 3 and 4 interfaces be up but have unassigned IP addresses?

Step 9

From DLSwitch, verify neighbors with CDP:

```
DLSwitch> (enable) show cdp neighbors
```

13. What are the neighboring devices and platforms? How does this resolve with the diagram at the beginning of the lab?

Step 10

Test your connections from ALSwitch. If you attempt pings outside of VLAN 1, they will likely fail. (Mixed results have been reported, depending on the 4006 operating systems.)

```
ALSwitch#ping 10.1.1.1
```

```
ALSwitch#ping 10.1.1.11
```

```
ALSwitch#ping 10.1.1.12
```

Step 11

Test your connections from DLSwitch. If you attempt pings outside of VLAN 1, they will likely fail. (Mixed results have been reported, depending on the 4006 operating systems.)

```
DLSwitch> (enable) ping 10.1.1.1


DLSwitch> (enable) ping 10.1.1.11


DLSwitch> (enable) ping 10.1.1.12
```

Step 12

Test your connections from DLRouter. If you attempt pings outside of VLAN 1, they will likely fail. (Mixed results have been reported, depending on the 4006 operating systems.)

```
DLRouter#ping 10.1.1.1

DLRouter#ping 10.1.1.11

DLRouter#ping 10.1.1.12
```

Step 13

From your workstation, test your network management capabilities:

Configure your workstation to IP address 10.1.1.2/24 using gateway 10.1.1.1, and connect it to any port on VLAN 1 on either the 2900 XL or 4006 switch. When connected, you should be able to ping and Telnet to all your networking devices:

- DLRouter at IP address 10.1.1.1
- ALSwitch at IP address 10.1.1.11
- DLSwitch at IP address 10.1.1.12

14. Can you communicate with other VLANs beyond VLAN 1?

This lab demonstrated the configuration of inter-VLAN routing with the 4006 L3 Services Module.

Lab 6-3: Routing Between the L3 Services Module and an External Router

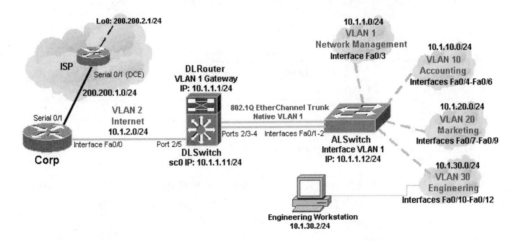

Objective

Configure routing between the L3 Services Module and an external router connected to an ISP.

Scenario

Current Environment

Your network switching equipment currently includes a Catalyst 4006 core switch and a 2900 XL access switch. Your network is segmented into four functional VLANs for better network management. They include "Accounting," "Marketing," and "Engineering" for the users and "default" for the native VLAN used for network management. Inter-VLAN routing has been implemented using a Layer 3 Services Module on the 4006 to allow individuals and servers on your VLANs to exchange information. VLAN trunking to the 2900 XL has been implemented over an FEC.

Enhancement

Your LAN functions well, and your company's executives have decided to implement outbound Internet connectivity using a 2600 series Cisco router connected as shown in the diagram. As part of this enhancement, you will establish a new VLAN named "Internet" with VLAN ID 2. This new VLAN will carry all Internet traffic for the local network. Other enhancements include the implementation of EIGRP between the 2600 series router and the 4006 L3 module and the enabling of VTP pruning on the DLSwitch for trunk optimization.

Design

The VTP and subnetwork information is as follows:

VTP configuration information:

Switch	VTP Domain	VTP Mode	VTP Pruning
DLSwitch	Corp	Server	Enabled
ALSwitch	Corp	Client	—

VLAN configuration information:

VLAN ID	VLAN Name	VLAN Subnet	VLAN Gateway
1	Default (native)	10.1.1.0/24	10.1.1.1
2	Internet	10.1.2.0/24	10.1.2.1
10	Accounting	10.1.10.0/24	10.1.10.1
20	Marketing	10.1.20.0/24	10.1.20.1
30	Engineering	10.1.30.0/24	10.1.30.1

Switch VLAN port/interface assignments:

Switch	VLAN 1	VLAN 2	VLAN 10	VLAN 20	VLAN 30	Trunk
DLSwitch	6 to 18	5	19 to 24	25 to 30	31 to 34	3 and 4
ALSwitch	3	—	4 to 6	7 to 9	10 to 12	1 and 2

Catalyst 4006 DLRouter interface configuration information:

Interface	IP Address	VLAN
PortChannel 1.1	10.1.1.1/24	Native 1
PortChannel 1.2	10.1.2.1/24	2
PortChannel 1.10	10.1.10.1/24	10
PortChannel 1.20	10.1.20.1/24	20
PortChannel 1.30	10.1.30.1/24	30

Cisco 2600 Internet router interface configuration information:

Interface	IP Address	NAT
Serial 0/0	—	—
Serial 0/1	200.200.1.2/24	Outside
FastEthernet 0/0	10.1.2.2/24	Inside
FastEthernet 0/1	—	—

Notes

_____

_____

_____

_____

_____

_____

_____

_____

_____

If you just completed Lab 6-2, "Configuring the L3 Services Module on a Catalyst 4006 Switch," you can skip to Step 8 to implement the enhancements outlined in this scenario. In Step 8 you verify that all components are functioning properly before you begin. If you are starting this lab without having completed the preceding lab, begin at Step 1 to configure your switched network foundation. Note, however, that Steps 1 through 7 do not explain the details as they were explained in the preceding lab.

Step 1

Cable the lab as shown in the diagram.

Step 2

The first device to be configured is the distribution layer switch, DLSwitch. Access it through the console port and enter privileged mode. Clear your NVRAM and reload:

```
Console> (enable) clear config all
Console> (enable) reset
```

Step 3

Configure DLSwitch with the following information:

a. Configure the system name DLSwitch on the Cisco 4006 switch:

```
Console> (enable) set system name DLSwitch
```

Note: Verify using **show config**.

b. Configure the VTP information on the 4006 switch. You will set the core switch as a VTP server, because pruning can be configured only on VTP servers:

```
DLSwitch> (enable) set vtp domain Corp
DLSwitch> (enable) set vtp mode server
```

Note: Verify using **show vtp domain**.

112

c. Create corporate VLANs:

```
DLSwitch> (enable) set vlan 1 name default
DLSwitch> (enable) set vlan 10 name Accounting
DLSwitch> (enable) set vlan 20 name Marketing
DLSwitch> (enable) set vlan 30 name Engineering
```

Note: Verify using **show vlan**.

d. Set switch IP address information and the VLAN 1 gateway:

```
DLSwitch (enable) set interface sc0 up
DLSwitch> (enable) set interface sc0 1 10.1.1.11/255.255.255.0 10.1.1.255
DLSwitch> (enable) set ip route 0.0.0.0/0.0.0.0 10.1.1.1
```

Note: Verify using **show config**.

e. (Optional) Set port channel admin groups:

```
DLSwitch> (enable) set port channel 2/1-2 156
DLSwitch> (enable) set port channel 2/3-4 157
```

Note: Verify using **show config**.

f. Assign port VLAN memberships:

```
DLSwitch> (enable) set vlan 10    2/19-24
DLSwitch >(enable) set vlan 20    2/25-30
DLSwitch >(enable) set vlan 30    2/31-34
```

Note: Verify using **show vlan**.

g. Establish VLAN trunking. These commands let you establish trunking to the 2900 XL and to the internal Gigabit interfaces on the L3 module:

```
DLSwitch> (enable) set trunk 2/1 nonegotiate dot1q 1-1005
DLSwitch> (enable) set trunk 2/2 nonegotiate dot1q 1-1005
DLSwitch> (enable) set trunk 2/3 nonegotiate dot1q 1-1005
DLSwitch> (enable) set trunk 2/4 nonegotiate dot1q 1-1005
```

Note: The **show trunk** command does not yet display useful trunk information, because the trunk links are not yet active.

h. Establish GEC and FEC on trunking interfaces:

```
DLSwitch> (enable) set port channel 2/1-2 mode on
DLSwitch> (enable) set port channel 2/3-4 mode on
```

Note: Verify using **show channel**.

i. Establish switch passwords. This lab uses **cisco** for all the passwords:

```
DLSwitch> (enable) set enablepass <enter>
```

You are prompted to enter and confirm the password:

```
DLSwitch> (enable) set password <enter>
```

You are prompted to enter and confirm the password.

j. Verify the complete configuration using **show config**.

Step 4

The next device to be configured is the access layer switch, ALSwitch. Access the switch through the console port, and enter privileged mode. Clear the NVRAM and reload. Deleting the vlan.dat file prevents the inadvertent propagation of unwanted VLAN information throughout the VTP domain:

```
Switch#delete vlan.dat
Switch#erase start
Switch#reload
```

Note: If you are asked whether you want to save system information, select **No**.

Step 5

Configure the ALSwitch switch with the following information:

a. Configure VTP trunking information. Remember that the **vtp domain** command is not actually necessary, because the name will be learned from the VTP server:

```
Switch#vlan database
Switch(vlan)#vtp client
Switch(vlan)#vtp domain Corp
Switch(vlan)#exit
```

b. Verify VTP information. It should look similar to the following:

```
Switch#show vtp stat

VTP Version                   : 2
Configuration Revision        : 7
Maximum VLANs supported locally : 68
Number of existing VLANs      : 8
VTP Operating Mode            : Client
VTP Domain Name               : Corp
VTP Pruning Mode              : Disabled
VTP V2 Mode                   : Disabled
VTP Traps Generation          : Disabled
MD5 digest                    : 0x32 0x9A 0x94 0x94 0x04 0x9E 0xDC 0x09
Configuration last modified by 0.0.0.0 at 3-1-93 00:47:02
```

c. Configure the host name, ALSwitch, on the 2900 XL switch:

```
Switch(config)#hostname ALSwitch
```

Note: Verify using **show run**.

d. Configure the privileged-mode password. All passwords for this lab are **cisco**:

```
ALSwitch(config)#enable password cisco
```

Note: Verify using **show run**.

e. Configure trunking and the FEC:

```
ALSwitch(config)#interface FastEthernet0/1
ALSwitch(config-if)#port group 1
ALSwitch(config-if)#switchport trunk encapsulation dot1q
ALSwitch(config-if)#switchport mode trunk

ALSwitch(config)#interface FastEthernet0/2
ALSwitch(config-if)#port group 1
ALSwitch(config-if)#switchport trunk encapsulation dot1q
ALSwitch(config-if)#switchport mode trunk
```

Note: Verify using **show run**.

f. Configure port VLAN memberships and spanning tree PortFast:

```
ALSwitch(config)#interface FastEthernet0/3
ALSwitch(config-if)#switchport access vlan 1
ALSwitch(config-if)#spanning-tree portfast

ALSwitch(config)#interface FastEthernet0/4
ALSwitch(config-if)#switchport access vlan 10
ALSwitch(config-if)#spanning-tree portfast

ALSwitch(config)#interface FastEthernet0/5
ALSwitch(config-if)#switchport access vlan 10
ALSwitch(config-if)#spanning-tree portfast

ALSwitch(config)#interface FastEthernet0/6
ALSwitch(config-if)#switchport access vlan 10
ALSwitch(config-if)#spanning-tree portfast

ALSwitch(config)#interface FastEthernet0/7
ALSwitch(config-if)#switchport access vlan 20
ALSwitch(config-if)#spanning-tree portfast

ALSwitch(config)#interface FastEthernet0/8
ALSwitch(config-if)#switchport access vlan 20
ALSwitch(config-if)#spanning-tree portfast

ALSwitch(config)#interface FastEthernet0/9
ALSwitch(config-if)#switchport access vlan 20
ALSwitch(config-if)#spanning-tree portfast
```

```
ALSwitch(config)#interface FastEthernet0/10
ALSwitch(config-if)#switchport access vlan 30
ALSwitch(config-if)#spanning-tree portfast

ALSwitch(config)#interface FastEthernet0/11
ALSwitch(config-if)#switchport access vlan 30
ALSwitch(config-if)#spanning-tree portfast

ALSwitch(config)#interface FastEthernet0/12
ALSwitch(config-if)#switchport access vlan 30
ALSwitch(config-if)#spanning-tree portfast
```

Note: Verify using **show run**.

g. Configure the VLAN 1 management interface IP address and default gateway for ALSwitch:

```
ALSwitch(config)#ip default-gateway 10.1.1.1

ALSwitch(config)#interface VLAN1
ALSwitch(config-if)#ip address 10.1.1.12 255.255.255.0
```

Note: Verify using **show run**.

h. Configure the password for the vty lines:

```
ALSwitch(config)#line vty 0 4
ALSwitch(config-line)#password cisco
ALSwitch(config-line)#login
```

i. Verify the complete configuration using **show run**.

Step 6

The next device to be configured is the distribution layer router, DLRouter. Access the Supervisor Engine II via the console port, and enter privileged mode. Clear your NVRAM and reload:

```
DLSwitch> (enable) session 2
Router#erase start
Router#reload
```

Note: If you are asked whether you want to save system information, select **No**.

After the card is reset, go back into it. This might take a few minutes.

```
DLSwitch> (enable) session 2
```

Step 7

Configure DLRouter with the following information:

a. Configure the host name, DLRouter, on the 4006 L3 module:

```
Router (config)#hostname DLRouter
```

Note: Verify using **show run**.

b. Configure the privileged-mode password:

```
DLRouter(config)#enable password cisco
```

Note: Verify using **show run**.

c. Configure the VLAN interface addressing and trunking encapsulation:

```
DLRouter(config)#interface Port-channel1
DLRouter(config-if)#ip address 10.1.1.1 255.255.255.0
DLRouter(config-if)#no shutdown

DLRouter(config)#interface Port-channel1.10
DLRouter(config-if)#encapsulation dot1Q 10
DLRouter(config-if)#ip address 10.1.10.1 255.255.255.0

DLRouter(config)#interface Port-channel1.20
DLRouter(config-if)#encapsulation dot1Q 20
DLRouter(config-if)#ip address 10.1.20.1 255.255.255.0

DLRouter(config)#interface Port-channel1.30
DLRouter(config-if)#encapsulation dot1Q 30
DLRouter(config-if)#ip address 10.1.30.1 255.255.255.0
```

Note: Verify using **show run**.

d. Assign the Gigabit interfaces to the port channel:

```
DLRouter(config)#interface GigabitEthernet3
DLRouter(config-if)#channel-group 1

DLRouter(config)#interface GigabitEthernet4
DLRouter(config-if)#channel-group 1
```

Note: Verify using **show run**.

e. Configure your corporate routing protocol:

```
DLRouter(config)#router eigrp 1
DLRouter(config-router)#network 10.0.0.0
```

Note: Verify using **show run**.

f. Configure your vty line password information:

```
DLRouter(config)#line vty 0 4
DLRouter(config-line)#password cisco
DLRouter(config-line)#login
```

g. Verify the complete configuration using **show run**.

Step 8

From DLRouter, verify your connection to DLSwitch through the port channel. The expected output is shown for verification, but yours will not match exactly:

```
DLRouter#show cdp neighbors

Capability Codes: R - Router, T - Trans Bridge, B - Source Route Bridge
                  S - Switch, H - Host, I - IGMP, r - Repeater
Device ID        Local Intrfce    Holdtme   Capability  Platform  Port
ID
JAB04290BND      Port-channel1     154          T S      WS-C4006  2/1
JAB04290BND      Port-channel1     154          T S      WS-C4006  2/2

DLRouter#show ip interface brief

Interface               IP-Address      OK? Method Status     Protocol
FX1000:1                unassigned      YES unset  up          up
FastEthernet1           unassigned      YES NVRAM  down        down
GigabitEthernet1        unassigned      YES NVRAM  down        down
GigabitEthernet2        unassigned      YES NVRAM  down        down
GigabitEthernet3        unassigned      YES NVRAM  up          up
GigabitEthernet4        unassigned      YES NVRAM  up          up
Controller5             unassigned      YES unset  up          up
Port-channel1           10.1.1.1        YES NVRAM  up          up
Port-channel1.10        10.1.10.1       YES NVRAM  up          up
Port-channel1.20        10.1.20.1       YES NVRAM  up          up
Port-channel1.30        10.1.30.1       YES NVRAM  up          up
```

Step 9

From DLSwitch, verify neighbors with CDP. The expected output is shown for verification. Yours might not match exactly:

```
DLSwitch> (enable) show cdp neighbors

* - indicates vlan mismatch.
# - indicates duplex mismatch.
Port      Device-ID               Port-ID               Platform
--------  ----------------------  --------------------  ------------
  2/1     DLRouter                GigabitEthernet3      cisco Cat4232
  2/2     DLRouter                GigabitEthernet4      cisco Cat4232
  2/2     DLRouter                Port-channel1         cisco Cat4232
  2/3     ALSwitch                FastEthernet0/1       cisco WS-C2912-XL
  2/4     ALSwitch                FastEthernet0/2       cisco WS-C2912-XL
```

Step 10

Test your connections from ALSwitch. The expected output is shown for verification. Yours might not match exactly:

```
ALSwitch#ping 10.1.1.1

Type escape sequence to abort.
Sending 5, 100-byte ICMP Echos to 10.1.1.1, timeout is 2 seconds:
!!!!!
Success rate is 100 percent (5/5), round-trip min/avg/max = 1/2/6 ms

ALSwitch#ping 10.1.1.11
```

```
Type escape sequence to abort.
Sending 5, 100-byte ICMP Echos to 10.1.1.11, timeout is 2 seconds:
!!!!!
Success rate is 100 percent (5/5), round-trip min/avg/max = 5/10/21 ms

ALSwitch#ping 10.1.1.12

Type escape sequence to abort.
Sending 5, 100-byte ICMP Echos to 10.1.1.12, timeout is 2 seconds:
!!!!!
Success rate is 100 percent (5/5), round-trip min/avg/max = 1/2/5 ms
```

Step 11

Test your connections from DLSwitch. The expected output is shown for
verification. Yours might not match exactly:

```
DLSwitch> (enable) ping 10.1.1.1

10.1.1.1 is alive

DLSwitch> (enable) ping 10.1.1.11

10.1.1.11 is alive

DLSwitch> (enable) ping 10.1.1.12

10.1.1.12 is alive
```

Step 12

Test your connections from DLRouter. The expected output is shown for
verification. Yours might not match exactly:

```
DLRouter#ping 10.1.1.1

Type escape sequence to abort.
Sending 5, 100-byte ICMP Echos to 10.1.1.1, timeout is 2 seconds:
!!!!!
Success rate is 100 percent (5/5), round-trip min/avg/max = 1/1/4 ms

DLRouter#ping 10.1.1.11

Type escape sequence to abort.
Sending 5, 100-byte ICMP Echos to 10.1.1.11, timeout is 2 seconds:
!!!!!
Success rate is 100 percent (5/5), round-trip min/avg/max = 4/7/8 ms

DLRouter#ping 10.1.1.12

Type escape sequence to abort.
Sending 5, 100-byte ICMP Echos to 10.1.1.12, timeout is 2 seconds:
!!!!!
Success rate is 100 percent (5/5), round-trip min/avg/max = 1/2/4 ms
```

Step 13

Now that the LAN is completely configured and tested, focus on the items that are required to add Internet connectivity to the local LAN by routing through the L3 module. First, let's take care of the DLSwitch:

a. Configure DLSwitch parameters for Internet connectivity and VLAN 2. With the following commands, you enable pruning for VLAN traffic optimization. You will add the "Internet" VLAN as VLAN 2. The Corp router will be connected to port 2/5 on the switch, so you will set that port to VLAN 2 and then enable PortFast for instant connectivity:

```
DLSwitch> (enable) set vtp pruning enable
DLSwitch> (enable) set vlan 2 name Internet
DLSwitch> (enable) set vlan 2 2/5
DLSwitch> (enable) set spantree portfast 2/5 enable
```

Note: Verify using **show config**.

b. Check the running configuration information for verification as well. Showing the VLANs lets you check that VLAN 2 was configured properly. It should appear like the other VLANs:

```
DLSwitch> (enable) show vlan
```

VLAN	Name	Status	IfIndex	Mod/Ports, Vlans
1	default	active	101	1/1-2
				2/6-18
2	Internet	active	111	2/5
10	Accounting	active	106	2/19-24
20	Marketing	active	107	2/25-30
30	Engineering	active	108	2/31-34
1002	fddi-default	active	102	
1003	token-ring-default	active	105	
1004	fddinet-default	active	103	
1005	trnet-default	active	104	

c. It is important now to verify the connectivity between the network devices. Assuming that items were configured properly, simply looking at CDP information reported by the neighbors lets you do exactly that:

```
DLSwitch> (enable) show cdp neighbor
```

Complete the following chart:

```
* - indicates vlan mismatch.
# - indicates duplex mismatch.
```

Port	Device-ID	Port-ID	Platform	
2/1	_____	GigabitEthernet3	cisco	_____
2/2	_____	GigabitEthernet4	cisco	_____
2/2	_____	Port-channel1	cisco	_____
2/3	_____	FastEthernet0/1	cisco	_____
2/4	_____	FastEthernet0/2	cisco	_____

d. Check the VTP configuration information. Because you enabled pruning, it should display as well:

```
DLSwitch> (enable) show vtp domain
```

Complete the following chart:

Domain Name	Domain Index	VTP Version	Local Mode	Password
_____	1	2	_____	-

Step 14

Next, you need to take care of DLRouter. Now that you have the VLAN information for VLAN 2 configured on DLSwitch, you simply need to add it to DLRouter's port channel to participate in inter-VLAN routing:

a. Configure DLRouter parameters:

```
DLRouter(config)#interface Port-channel1.2
DLRouter(config-if)#encapsulation dot1Q 2
DLRouter(config-if)#ip address 10.1.2.1 255.255.255.0
```

Note: Verify using **show run**.

b. Issue some commands to verify the DLRouter operation. You'll check the active interfaces and take a look at the neighbors. Make sure that the new VLAN is routing and active. Enter the following commands:

```
DLRouter#show cdp neighbor
```

Complete the following chart:

```
Capability Codes: R - Router, T - Trans Bridge, B - Source Route Bridge
                  S - Switch, H - Host, I - IGMP, r - Repeater
Device ID          Local Intrfce    Holdtme    Capability  Platform  Port ID
JAB04290BND(DLSSwPort-channel1       144          T S       _____ _____
JAB04290BND(DLSSwPort-channel1       144          T S       _____ _____
```

```
DLRouter#show ip interface brief
```

1. Does the output from this command illustrate that VLAN 2 is active?

_____

Step 15

Now that the VLAN information for VLAN 2 is configured on DLSwitch and DLRouter, your next step is to configure the Corp router. This router will be connected to the DLSwitch on port 2/5.

a. Clear your NVRAM and reload:

```
Router#erase start
Router#reload
```

Note: If you are asked whether you want to save system information, select **No**.

b. Configure the router with the following information. As you can see, you use basic NAT for the address translation from private to public addresses, and you use EIGRP to propagate the default route and network communication to the DLRouter. Everything else is fairly standard, such as the host name, passwords, and default static route to the Internet:

```
Router(config)# hostname Corp
Corp(config)# enable password cisco

Corp(config)# interface FastEthernet0/0
Corp(config-if)# ip address 10.1.2.2 255.255.255.0
Corp(config-if)# ip nat inside
Corp(config-if)# no shutdown

Corp(config)# interface Serial0/1
Corp(config-if)# ip address 200.200.1.2 255.255.255.0
Corp(config-if)# ip nat outside
Corp(config-if)# no shutdown

Corp(config)# router eigrp 1
Corp(config-router)# redistribute static metric 64 20000 255 1 1500
Corp(config-router)# passive-interface Serial0/1
Corp(config-router)# network 10.0.0.0

Corp(config)# ip route 0.0.0.0 0.0.0.0 200.200.1.1

Corp(config)# ip nat inside source list 1 interface Serial0/1 overload
Corp(config)# access-list 1 permit any

Corp(config)# line vty 0 4
Corp(config-line)# password cisco
Corp(config-line)# login
```

Note: Verify using **show run** and **show ip interface brief**.

c. Check some of the configurations. Note that you should see the DLSwitch as a neighbor and the EIGRP routing updates as well. Also, go back to the DLRouter and view the routing table. You should see the gateway of last resort being advertised from the Corp router, as shown here:

```
Corp#show cdp neighbor

Capability Codes: R - Router, T - Trans Bridge, B - Source Route Bridge
                  S - Switch, H - Host, I - IGMP, r - Repeater
Device ID      Local Intrfce    Holdtme    Capability  Platform  Port ID
JAB04290BND(DLSSwFas 0/0            139          T S       WS-C4006  2/5

Corp#show ip route
```

Complete the following chart:

```
Codes: C - connected, S - static, I - IGRP, R - RIP, M - mobile, B - BGP
       D - EIGRP, EX - EIGRP external, O - OSPF, IA - OSPF inter area
       N1 - OSPF NSSA external type 1, N2 - OSPF NSSA external type 2
       E1 - OSPF external type 1, E2 - OSPF external type 2, E - EGP
       i - IS-IS, L1 - IS-IS level-1, L2 - IS-IS level-2, ia - IS-IS area
       * - candidate default, U - per-user static route, o - ODR
       P - periodic downloaded static route

Gateway of last resort is _____ to network 0.0.0.0

____   200.200.1.0/24 is directly connected, Serial0/1
       10.0.0.0/24 is subnetted, 5 subnets
____      10.1.10.0 [90/28416] via 10.1.2.1, 01:10:14, FastEthernet0/0
____      10.1.2.0 is directly connected, FastEthernet0/0
____      10.1.1.0 [90/28416] via 10.1.2.1, 01:10:14, FastEthernet0/0
____      10.1.30.0 [90/28416] via 10.1.2.1, 01:10:14, FastEthernet0/0
____      10.1.20.0 [90/28416] via 10.1.2.1, 01:10:14, FastEthernet0/0
S*     0.0.0.0/0 [1/0] via _____


         DLRouter#show ip route
```

2. Is the gateway of last resort established via EIGRP automatically? If so, how do you know this? _____

Step 16

The next device to be configured is the ISP router:

a. Clear your NVRAM and reload:

```
Router#erase start
Router#reload
```

Note: If you are asked whether you want to save system information, select **No**.

b. Configure the ISP router as follows, and verify communication:

```
Router(config)#hostname ISP

ISP(config)#interface Loopback0
ISP(config-if)# ip address 200.200.2.1 255.255.255.0

ISP(config)#interface Serial0/1
ISP(config-if)# ip address 200.200.1.1 255.255.255.0
ISP(config-if)# clockrate 56000
ISP(config-if)# no shutdown
```

Note: Verify using **show run** and **show ip interface brief**.

Step 17

Finally, do some testing:

a. Try to ping the ISP router from the DLRouter first:

```
DLRouter>ping 200.200.2.1

Type escape sequence to abort.
Sending 5, 100-byte ICMP Echos to 200.200.2.1, timeout is 2 seconds:
!!!!!
Success rate is 100 percent (5/5), round-trip min/avg/max = 32/32/36 ms
```

b. Connect and configure workstations on different VLANs, and verify Internet connectivity.

This lab demonstrated how to configure inter-VLAN routing between a Catalyst 4006 L3 Services Module and external routers connected to the Internet.

124

Lab 6-4: IP Helper Addresses for DHCP Relay on an L3 Services Module

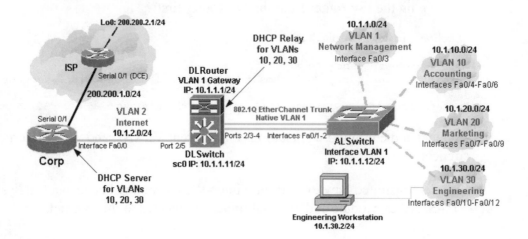

Objective

Configure an IP helper address pointing to a router configured as a DHCP server.

Scenario

Current Environment

Your network equipment currently includes a Catalyst 4006 core switch, a Catalyst 2900 XL access switch, and a Cisco 2600 series Internet router. Your network is segmented into five functional VLANs. They include "Accounting," "Marketing," "Engineering," and "Internet" for users, and "default," the native VLAN used for network management. Inter-VLAN routing is implemented with a Layer 3 Services Module on the 4006 to allow individuals and servers on your VLANs to exchange information. VLAN trunking to the 2900 XL is implemented over an FEC. EIGRP is configured between the 2600 series router and the 4006 L3 module. VTP pruning is enabled on DLSwitch for VLAN trunk optimization.

Enhancement

The desktop support staff reports that static IP addressing is cumbersome and inefficient. They have requested that, as the network engineer, you implement dynamic addressing with DHCP. After gaining management approval, you decide to implement dynamic addressing for VLANs 10, 20, and 30 only, because the others do not require it. Additionally, the first 25 addresses in each range should be excluded from the scopes for servers and printers. You select the 2600 to support the scopes, because your current IOS on DLRouter will not allow it to act as a DHCP server. Hence, each VLAN interface must relay DHCP requests to the 2600 router to fulfill DHCP requests.

Design

The VTP and subnetwork information is as follows:

VTP configuration information:

Switch	VTP Domain	VTP Mode	VTP Pruning
DLSwitch	Corp	Server	Enabled
ALSwitch	Corp	Client	—

VLAN configuration information:

VLAN ID	VLAN Name	VLAN Subnet	VLAN Gateway
1	default (native)	10.1.1.0/24	10.1.1.1
2	Internet	10.1.2.0/24	10.1.2.1
10	Accounting	10.1.10.0/24	10.1.10.1
20	Marketing	10.1.20.0/24	10.1.20.1
30	Engineering	10.1.30.0/24	10.1.30.1

Switch VLAN port/interface assignments:

Switch	VLAN 1	VLAN 2	VLAN 10	VLAN 20	VLAN 30	Trunk
DLSwitch	6 to 18	5	19 to 24	25 to 30	31 to 34	3 and 4
ALSwitch	3	—	4 to 6	7 to 9	10 to 12	1 and 2

Catalyst 4006 DLRouter interface configuration information:

Interface	IP Address	VLAN
PortChannel 1.1	10.1.1.1/24	Native 1
PortChannel 1.2	10.1.2.1/24	2
PortChannel 1.10	10.1.10.1/24	10
PortChannel 1.20	10.1.20.1/24	20
PortChannel 1.30	10.1.30.1/24	30

Cisco 2600 Internet router interface configuration information:

Interface	IP Address	NAT
Serial 0/0	—	—
Serial 0/1	200.200.1.2/24	Outside
FastEthernet 0/0	10.1.2.2/24	Inside
FastEthernet 0/1	—	—

Notes

_____

_____

_____

If you completed Lab 6-3, "Routing Between the L3 Services Module and an External Router," you are ready to implement the DHCP VLAN processes in the same network environment. In this case, skip to Step 17. In Step 17 you verify that all components are functioning properly before you begin. If you didn't complete the preceding lab, begin at Step 1. We will not expend time on task explanations through Step 18, because that was done in previous labs.

Step 1

Cable the lab as shown in the diagram.

Step 2

The first device to be configured is the distribution layer switch, DLSwitch. Access the switch through the console port, and enter privileged mode. Clear your NVRAM and reload:

```
Console> (enable) clear config all
Console> (enable) reset
```

Step 3

Configure DLSwitch with the following information:

a. Configure the system name, DLSwitch, on the Cisco 4006 switch:

```
Console> (enable) set system name DLSwitch
```

Note: Verify using **show config**.

b. Configure the VTP information on the 4006 switch. You will set the core switch as a VTP server, because pruning can be configured only on VTP servers:

```
DLSwitch> (enable) set vtp domain Corp
DLSwitch> (enable) set vtp mode server
```

Note: Verify using **show vtp domain**.

c. Create corporate VLANs:

```
DLSwitch> (enable) set vlan 1 name default
DLSwitch> (enable) set vlan 10 name Accounting
DLSwitch> (enable) set vlan 20 name Marketing
DLSwitch> (enable) set vlan 30 name Engineering
```

Note: Verify using **show vlan**.

d. Set switch IP address information and the VLAN 1 gateway:

```
DLSwitch> (enable) set interface sc0 up
DLSwitch> (enable) set interface sc0 1 10.1.1.11/255.255.255.0
10.1.1.255
DLSwitch> (enable) set ip route 0.0.0.0/0.0.0.0 10.1.1.1
```

Note: Verify using **show config**.

e. (Optional) Set port channel admin groups:

```
DLSwitch> (enable) set port channel 2/1-2 156
DLSwitch> (enable) set port channel 2/3-4 157
```

Note: Verify using **show config**.

f. Assign port VLAN memberships:

```
DLSwitch> (enable) set vlan 10   2/19-24
DLSwitch >(enable) set vlan 20   2/25-30
DLSwitch >(enable) set vlan 30   2/31-34
```

Note: Verify using **show vlan**.

g. Establish VLAN trunking. These commands let you establish trunking to the 2900 XL and to the internal Gigabit interfaces on the L3 module:

```
DLSwitch> (enable) set trunk 2/1 nonegotiate dot1q 1-1005
DLSwitch> (enable) set trunk 2/2 nonegotiate dot1q 1-1005
DLSwitch> (enable) set trunk 2/3 nonegotiate dot1q 1-1005
DLSwitch> (enable) set trunk 2/4 nonegotiate dot1q 1-1005
```

Note: The **show trunk** command does not yet display useful trunk information, because the trunk links are not yet active.

h. Establish GEC and FEC on trunking interfaces:

```
DLSwitch> (enable) set port channel 2/1-2 mode on
DLSwitch> (enable) set port channel 2/3-4 mode on
```

Note: Verify using **show channel**.

i. Establish switch passwords. The password **cisco** is used throughout this lab:

```
DLSwitch> (enable) set enablepass <enter>
```

You are prompted to enter and confirm the password:

```
DLSwitch> (enable) set password <enter>
```

You are prompted to enter and confirm the password.

j. Verify the complete configuration using **show config**.

Step 4

The next device to be configured is the access layer switch, ALSwitch. Access the switch through the console port, and enter privileged mode. Clear the NVRAM and reload. Deleting the vlan.dat file prevents the inadvertent propagation of unwanted VLAN information throughout the VTP domain:

```
Switch#delete vlan.dat
Switch#erase start
Switch#reload
```

Note: If you are asked whether you want to save system information, select **No**.

Step 5

Configure ALSwitch with the following information:

a. Configure VTP trunking information. Note that the **vtp domain** command is not really necessary, because the VTP domain name is learned from the VTP server.

```
Switch#vlan database
Switch(vlan)#vtp client
Switch(vlan)#vtp domain Corp
Switch(vlan)#exit
```

b. Verify VTP information. It should look similar to the following:

```
Switch#show vtp stat

VTP Version                   : 2
Configuration Revision        : 7
Maximum VLANs supported locally : 68
Number of existing VLANs      : 8
VTP Operating Mode            : Client
VTP Domain Name               : Corp
VTP Pruning Mode              : Disabled
VTP V2 Mode                   : Disabled
VTP Traps Generation          : Disabled
MD5 digest                    : 0x32 0x9A 0x94 0x94 0x04 0x9E 0xDC 0x09
Configuration last modified by 0.0.0.0 at 3-1-93 00:47:02
```

c. Configure the host name, ALSwitch, on the 2900 XL switch:

```
Switch(config)#hostname ALSwitch
```

Note: Verify using **show run**.

d. Configure the privileged-mode password. All passwords for this lab are **cisco**:

```
ALSwitch(config)#enable password cisco
```

Note: Verify using **show run**.

e. Configure trunking and the FEC:

```
ALSwitch(config)#interface FastEthernet0/1
ALSwitch(config-if)#port group 1
ALSwitch(config-if)#switchport trunk encapsulation dot1q
ALSwitch(config-if)#switchport mode trunk

ALSwitch(config)#interface FastEthernet0/2
ALSwitch(config-if)#port group 1
ALSwitch(config-if)#switchport trunk encapsulation dot1q
ALSwitch(config-if)#switchport mode trunk
```

Note: Verify using **show run**.

f. Configure port VLAN memberships and spanning tree PortFast:

```
ALSwitch(config)#interface FastEthernet0/3
ALSwitch(config-if)#switchport access vlan 1
ALSwitch(config-if)#spanning-tree portfast

ALSwitch(config)#interface FastEthernet0/4
ALSwitch(config-if)#switchport access vlan 10
ALSwitch(config-if)#spanning-tree portfast

ALSwitch(config)#interface FastEthernet0/5
ALSwitch(config-if)#switchport access vlan 10
ALSwitch(config-if)#spanning-tree portfast

ALSwitch(config)#interface FastEthernet0/6
ALSwitch(config-if)#switchport access vlan 10
ALSwitch(config-if)#spanning-tree portfast

ALSwitch(config)#interface FastEthernet0/7
ALSwitch(config-if)#switchport access vlan 20
ALSwitch(config-if)#spanning-tree portfast

ALSwitch(config)#interface FastEthernet0/8
ALSwitch(config-if)#switchport access vlan 20
ALSwitch(config-if)#spanning-tree portfast

ALSwitch(config)#interface FastEthernet0/9
ALSwitch(config-if)#switchport access vlan 20
ALSwitch(config-if)#spanning-tree portfast

ALSwitch(config)#interface FastEthernet0/10
ALSwitch(config-if)#switchport access vlan 30
ALSwitch(config-if)#spanning-tree portfast

ALSwitch(config)#interface FastEthernet0/11
ALSwitch(config-if)#switchport access vlan 30
ALSwitch(config-if)#spanning-tree portfast

ALSwitch(config)#interface FastEthernet0/12
ALSwitch(config-if)#switchport access vlan 30
ALSwitch(config-if)#spanning-tree portfast
```

Note: Verify using **show run**.

g. Configure the VLAN 1 management interface IP address and default gateway for ALSwitch:

```
ALSwitch(config)#ip default-gateway 10.1.1.1

ALSwitch(config)#interface VLAN1
ALSwitch(config-if)#ip address 10.1.1.12 255.255.255.0
```

Note: Verify using **show run**.

h. Configure the password for the vty lines:

```
ALSwitch(config)#line vty 0 4
ALSwitch(config-line)#password cisco
ALSwitch(config-line)#login
```

i. Verify the complete configuration using **show run**.

Step 6

The next device to be configured is the distribution layer router, DLRouter. Access the Supervisor Engine II via the console port, and enter privileged mode. Clear your NVRAM and reload:

```
DLSwitch> (enable) session 2
Router#erase start
Router#reload
```

Note: If you are asked whether you want to save system information, select **No**.

After the card is reset, go back into it. This might take a few minutes.

```
DLSwitch> (enable) session 2
```

Step 7

Configure DLRouter with the following information:

a. Configure the host name, DLRouter, on the 4006 L3 module:

```
Router (config)#hostname DLRouter
```

Note: Verify using **show run**.

b. Configure the privileged-mode password:

```
DLRouter(config)#enable password cisco
```

Note: Verify using **show run**.

c. Configure the VLAN interface addressing and trunking encapsulation:

```
DLRouter(config)#interface Port-channel1
DLRouter(config-if)#ip address 10.1.1.1 255.255.255.0
DLRouter(config-if)#no shutdown

DLRouter(config)#interface Port-channel1.10
DLRouter(config-if)#encapsulation dot1Q 10
DLRouter(config-if)#ip address 10.1.10.1 255.255.255.0

DLRouter(config)#interface Port-channel1.20
DLRouter(config-if)#encapsulation dot1Q 20
DLRouter(config-if)#ip address 10.1.20.1 255.255.255.0

DLRouter(config)#interface Port-channel1.30
DLRouter(config-if)#encapsulation dot1Q 30
DLRouter(config-if)#ip address 10.1.30.1 255.255.255.0
```

Note: Verify using **show run**.

d. Assign the Gigabit interfaces to the port channel:

```
DLRouter(config)#interface GigabitEthernet3
DLRouter(config-if)#channel-group 1

DLRouter(config)#interface GigabitEthernet4
DLRouter(config-if)#channel-group 1
```

Note: Verify using **show run**.

e. Configure your corporate routing protocol:

```
DLRouter(config)#router eigrp 1
DLRouter(config-router)#network 10.0.0.0
```

Note: Verify using **show run**.

f. Configure your vty line password information:

```
DLRouter(config)#line vty 0 4
DLRouter(config-line)#password cisco
DLRouter(config-line)#login
```

g. Verify the complete configuration using **show run**.

Step 8

From DLRouter, verify your connection to DLSwitch through the port channel. The expected output is shown for verification, but yours will not match exactly:

```
DLRouter#show cdp neighbors

Capability Codes: R - Router, T - Trans Bridge, B - Source Route Bridge
                  S - Switch, H - Host, I - IGMP, r - Repeater
Device ID      Local Intrfce    Holdtme   Capability  Platform  Port ID
```

```
JAB04290BND        Port-channel1       154            T S        WS-C4006  2/1
JAB04290BND        Port-channel1       154            T S        WS-C4006  2/2

DLRouter#show ip interface brief

Interface               IP-Address      OK? Method Status     Protocol
FX1000:1                unassigned      YES unset  up         up
FastEthernet1           unassigned      YES NVRAM  down       down
GigabitEthernet1        unassigned      YES NVRAM  down       down
GigabitEthernet2        unassigned      YES NVRAM  down       down
GigabitEthernet3        unassigned      YES NVRAM  up         up
GigabitEthernet4        unassigned      YES NVRAM  up         up
Controller5             unassigned      YES unset  up         up
Port-channel1           10.1.1.1        YES NVRAM  up         up
Port-channel1.10        10.1.10.1       YES NVRAM  up         up
Port-channel1.20        10.1.20.1       YES NVRAM  up         up
Port-channel1.30        10.1.30.1       YES NVRAM  up         up
```

Step 9

From DLSwitch, verify neighbors with CDP. The expected output is shown for verification. Yours might not match exactly:

```
DLSwitch> (enable) show cdp neighbors

* - indicates vlan mismatch.
# - indicates duplex mismatch.
Port     Device-ID               Port-ID               Platform
-------- --------------------    ----------------------  ------------
  2/1    DLRouter                GigabitEthernet3        cisco Cat4232
  2/2    DLRouter                GigabitEthernet4        cisco Cat4232
  2/2    DLRouter                Port-channel1           cisco Cat4232
  2/3    ALSwitch                FastEthernet0/1         cisco WS-C2912-XL
  2/4    ALSwitch                FastEthernet0/2         cisco WS-C2912-XL
```

Step 10

Test your connections from ALSwitch. The expected output is shown for verification. Yours might not match exactly:

```
ALSwitch#ping 10.1.1.1

Type escape sequence to abort.
Sending 5, 100-byte ICMP Echos to 10.1.1.1, timeout is 2 seconds:
!!!!!
Success rate is 100 percent (5/5), round-trip min/avg/max = 1/2/6 ms

ALSwitch#ping 10.1.1.11

Type escape sequence to abort.
Sending 5, 100-byte ICMP Echos to 10.1.1.11, timeout is 2 seconds:
!!!!!
Success rate is 100 percent (5/5), round-trip min/avg/max = 5/10/21 ms

ALSwitch#ping 10.1.1.12

Type escape sequence to abort.
Sending 5, 100-byte ICMP Echos to 10.1.1.12, timeout is 2 seconds:
!!!!!
Success rate is 100 percent (5/5), round-trip min/avg/max = 1/2/5 ms
```

Step 11

Test your connections from DLSwitch. The expected output is shown for verification. Yours might not match exactly:

```
DLSwitch> (enable) ping 10.1.1.1

10.1.1.1 is alive

DLSwitch> (enable) ping 10.1.1.11

10.1.1.11 is alive

DLSwitch> (enable) ping 10.1.1.12

10.1.1.12 is alive
```

Step 12

Test your connections from DLRouter. The expected output is shown for verification. Yours might not match exactly:

```
DLRouter#ping 10.1.1.1

Type escape sequence to abort.
Sending 5, 100-byte ICMP Echos to 10.1.1.1, timeout is 2 seconds:
!!!!!
Success rate is 100 percent (5/5), round-trip min/avg/max = 1/1/4 ms

DLRouter#ping 10.1.1.11

Type escape sequence to abort.
Sending 5, 100-byte ICMP Echos to 10.1.1.11, timeout is 2 seconds:
!!!!!
Success rate is 100 percent (5/5), round-trip min/avg/max = 4/7/8 ms

DLRouter#ping 10.1.1.12

Type escape sequence to abort.
Sending 5, 100-byte ICMP Echos to 10.1.1.12, timeout is 2 seconds:
!!!!!
Success rate is 100 percent (5/5), round-trip min/avg/max = 1/2/4 ms
```

Step 13

Now that the LAN is completely configured and tested, you will focus on the items that are required to add Internet connectivity to the local LAN by routing through the L3 module. First, let's take care of the DLSwitch:

a. Configure DLSwitch parameters for Internet connectivity and VLAN 2. The following commands enable pruning for VLAN traffic optimization. You will add the "Internet" VLAN as VLAN 2. The Corp router will be connected to port 2/5 on the switch, so you will set that port to VLAN 2 and then enable PortFast for instant connectivity:

```
DLSwitch> (enable) set vtp pruning enable
DLSwitch> (enable) set vlan 2 name Internet
DLSwitch> (enable) set vlan 2 2/5
DLSwitch> (enable) set spantree portfast 2/5 enable
```

Note: Verify using **show config**.

b. Check the running configuration information as well for verification. Showing the VLANs lets you check that VLAN 2 was configured properly. It should appear like the other VLANs:

```
DLSwitch> (enable) show vlan

VLAN Name                        Status     IfIndex Mod/Ports, Vlans
---- --------------------------- ---------- ------- -----------------
1    default                     active     101     1/1-2
                                                     2/6-18
2    Internet                    active     111     2/5
10   Accounting                  active     106     2/19-24
20   Marketing                   active     107     2/25-30
30   Engineering                 active     108     2/31-34
1002 fddi-default                active     102
1003 token-ring-default          active     105
1004 fddinet-default             active     103
1005 trnet-default               active     104
```

c. It is important now to verify the connectivity between the network devices. Assuming that everything was configured properly, simply looking at CDP information reported by the neighbors lets you do exactly that:

```
DLSwitch> (enable) show cdp neighbor
```

Complete the following chart:

```
* - indicates vlan mismatch.
# - indicates duplex mismatch.
Port     Device-ID                          Port-ID              Platform
-------- ---------------------------------- -------------------- ------------
2/1      _____                          GigabitEthernet3     cisco _____
2/2      _____                          GigabitEthernet4     cisco _____
2/2      _____                          Port-channel1        cisco _____
2/3      _____                          FastEthernet0/1      cisco _____
2/4      _____                          FastEthernet0/2      cisco _____
```

d. Check the VTP configuration information. Because you enabled pruning, it should display as well:

```
DLSwitch> (enable) show vtp domain
```

Complete the following chart:

Domain Name	Domain Index	VTP Version	Local Mode	Password
_____	1	2	_____	-

Step 14

Next, you configure DLRouter. Now that you have the VLAN information for VLAN 2 configured on DLSwitch, you simply need to add it to DLRouter's port channel to participate in inter-VLAN routing.

135

a. Configure DLRouter parameters:

```
DLRouter(config)#interface Port-channel1.2
DLRouter(config-if)#encapsulation dot1Q 2
DLRouter(config-if)#ip address 10.1.2.1 255.255.255.0
```

Note: Verify using **show run**.

b. Issue some commands to verify the DLRouter operation. You'll check the active interfaces and take a look at the neighbors. Make sure that the new VLAN is routing and active. Enter the following commands:

```
DLRouter#show cdp neighbor
```

Complete the following chart:

```
Capability Codes: R - Router, T - Trans Bridge, B - Source Route Bridge
                  S - Switch, H - Host, I - IGMP, r - Repeater
Device ID          Local Intrfce     Holdtme    Capability Platform  Port ID
JAB04290BND(DLSSwPort-channel1        144           T S    _____  _____
JAB04290BND(DLSSwPort-channel1        144           T S    _____  _____
```

```
DLRouter#show ip interface brief
```

1. Does the output from this command illustrate that VLAN 2 is active?

_____

Step 15

Now that you have the VLAN information for VLAN 2 configured on DLSwitch and DLRouter, the next step is to configure the Corp router. This router will be connected to the DLSwitch on port 2/5:

a. Clear your NVRAM and reload:

```
Router#erase start
Router#reload
```

Note: If you are asked whether you want to save system information, select **No**.

b. Configure the router with the following information. As you can see, you use basic NAT for the address translation from private to public addresses, and you use EIGRP to propagate the default route and network communication to the DLRouter. Everything else is fairly standard, such as the host name, passwords, and default static route to the Internet:

```
Router(config)# hostname Corp
Corp(config)# enable password cisco

Corp(config)# interface FastEthernet0/0
Corp(config-if)# ip address 10.1.2.2 255.255.255.0
Corp(config-if)# ip nat inside
Corp(config-if)# no shutdown
```

```
Corp(config)# interface Serial0/1
Corp(config-if)# ip address 200.200.1.2 255.255.255.0
Corp(config-if)# ip nat outside
Corp(config-if)# no shutdown

Corp(config)# router eigrp 1
Corp(config-router)# redistribute static metric 64 20000 255 1 1500
Corp(config-router)# passive-interface Serial0/1
Corp(config-router)# network 10.0.0.0

Corp(config)# ip route 0.0.0.0 0.0.0.0 200.200.1.1

Corp(config)# ip nat inside source list 1 interface Serial0/1 overload
Corp(config)# access-list 1 permit any

Corp(config)# line vty 0 4
Corp(config-line)# password cisco
Corp(config-line)# login
```

Note: Verify using **show run** and **show ip interface brief**.

c. Check some of the configurations. Take special note that you should see DLSwitch as a neighbor and the EIGRP routing updates as well. Also, go back to the DLRouter and view the routing table. You should see the gateway of last resort being advertised from the Corp router as shown here:

```
Corp#show cdp neighbor

Capability Codes: R - Router, T - Trans Bridge, B - Source Route Bridge
                  S - Switch, H - Host, I - IGMP, r - Repeater
Device ID      Local Intrfce   Holdtme   Capability   Platform   Port ID
JAB04290BND(DLSSwFas 0/0          139          T S      WS-C4006   2/5

Corp#show ip route
```

Complete the following chart:

```
Codes: C - connected, S - static, I - IGRP, R - RIP, M - mobile, B - BGP
       D - EIGRP, EX - EIGRP external, O - OSPF, IA - OSPF inter area
       N1 - OSPF NSSA external type 1, N2 - OSPF NSSA external type 2
       E1 - OSPF external type 1, E2 - OSPF external type 2, E - EGP
       i - IS-IS, L1 - IS-IS level-1, L2 - IS-IS level-2, ia - IS-IS area
       * - candidate default, U - per-user static route, o - ODR
       P - periodic downloaded static route

Gateway of last resort is _____ to network 0.0.0.0

____  200.200.1.0/24 is directly connected, Serial0/1
      10.0.0.0/24 is subnetted, 5 subnets
____      10.1.10.0 [90/28416] via 10.1.2.1, 01:10:14, FastEthernet0/0
____      10.1.2.0 is directly connected, FastEthernet0/0
____      10.1.1.0 [90/28416] via 10.1.2.1, 01:10:14, FastEthernet0/0
____      10.1.30.0 [90/28416] via 10.1.2.1, 01:10:14, FastEthernet0/0
____      10.1.20.0 [90/28416] via 10.1.2.1, 01:10:14, FastEthernet0/0
S*    0.0.0.0/0 [1/0] via _____


      DLRouter#show ip route
```

2. Is the gateway of last resort established via EIGRP automatically? If so, how do you
know this? _____

Step 16

The next device to be configured is the ISP router:

a. Clear your NVRAM and reload:

```
Router#erase start
Router#reload
```

Note: If you are asked whether you want to save system information, select
No.

b. Configure the ISP router as follows, and verify communication:

```
Router(config)#hostname ISP

ISP(config)#interface Loopback0
ISP(config-if)# ip address 200.200.2.1 255.255.255.0

ISP(config)#interface Serial0/1
ISP(config-if)# ip address 200.200.1.1 255.255.255.0
ISP(config-if)# clockrate 56000
ISP(config-if)# no shutdown
```

Note: Verify using **show run** and **show ip interface brief**.

Step 17

Finally, you need to do some testing:

a. Try to ping the ISP router from the DLRouter first:

```
DLRouter>ping 200.200.2.1

Type escape sequence to abort.
Sending 5, 100-byte ICMP Echos to 200.200.2.1, timeout is 2 seconds:
!!!!!
Success rate is 100 percent (5/5), round-trip min/avg/max = 32/32/36 ms
```

b. Connect and configure workstations on different VLANs, and verify Internet
connectivity.

Step 18

Now, configure dynamic addressing (DHCP) for VLAN clients. Dynamic
addressing lets DHCP clients automatically acquire an IP address from the network
specifically for the VLAN they are connected to. This process is fairly simple in
that a DHCP pool needs to be created or hosted on a DHCP server, and all requests
must be relayed from the VLAN router to the configured server. Often, it is the case
that the VLAN router also hosts the DHCP requests, but more frequently an
external device such as a router or network server (a Windows 2000 box or UNIX
box) supports this function.

First, configure the DHCP services. For this role, you will choose the Corp router. This lab illustrates the DHCP relay configuration on the DLRouter. From the Corp router, enter the following commands:

```
Corp(config)#ip dhcp excluded-address 10.1.10.1 10.1.10.25
Corp(config)#ip dhcp excluded-address 10.1.20.1 10.1.20.25
Corp(config)#ip dhcp excluded-address 10.1.30.1 10.1.30.25

Corp(config)#ip dhcp pool VLAN10-Accounting
Corp(config-dhcp)#network 10.1.10.0 255.255.255.0
Corp(config-dhcp)#default-router 10.1.10.1

Corp(config)#ip dhcp pool VLAN20-Marketing
Corp(config-dhcp)#network 10.1.20.0 255.255.255.0
Corp(config-dhcp)#default-router 10.1.20.1

Corp(config)#ip dhcp pool VLAN30-Engineering
Corp(config-dhcp)#network 10.1.30.0 255.255.255.0
Corp(config-dhcp)#default-router 10.1.30.1
```

Note: Verify using **show run**.

Next, configure the port channel to relay the DHCP client requests to the DHCP server established on Corp. From DLRouter, enter the following commands:

```
DLRouter(config)#interface Port-channel1.10
DLRouter(config-if)#ip helper-address 10.1.2.2

DLRouter(config)#interface Port-channel1.20
DLRouter(config-if)#ip helper-address 10.1.2.2

DLRouter(config)#interface Port-channel1.30
DLRouter(config-if)#ip helper-address 10.1.2.2
```

Note: Verify using **show run**.

Step 19

Now, do some testing. This won't be fancy, but you should test some of the basic configurations:

a. Plug a workstation into a port on VLAN 10. Use **winipcfg** or **ipconfig** (depending on your version of the Microsoft Windows operating system) to release and renew the address. Remember that, if PortFast is not enabled, you might have to wait a minute or so after the workstation is connected.

3. What is your new address?

_____

4. Can you ping 200.200.2.1?

_____

5. Release and renew again. Was the DHCP process faster? Was your allocated IP address the same?

_____

b. Connect your workstation to a port on VLAN 30. Now, repeat the process for VLAN 30.

6. What is your new address?

_____

7. Can you ping 200.200.2.1?

_____

8. Release and renew again. Was the DHCP process faster? Was your allocated IP address the same?

_____

c. View the DHCP information. From the Corp router, enter the following commands, and look for the displayed results. Fill in the blanks:

Corp#**show ip dhcp bind**

IP address	Hardware address	Lease expiration	Type
_____	_____	_____	_____
_____	_____	_____	_____
_____	_____	_____	_____
_____	_____	_____	_____

Corp#**show ip dhcp server stat**

```
Memory usage            _____
Address pools           _____
Database agents         _____
Automatic bindings      _____
Manual bindings         _____
Expired bindings        _____
Malformed messages      _____

Message          Received
BOOTREQUEST        _____
DHCPDISCOVER       _____
DHCPREQUEST        _____
DHCPDECLINE        _____
DHCPRELEASE        _____
DHCPINFORM         _____

Message          Sent
BOOTREPLY          _____
DHCPOFFER          _____
DHCPACK            _____
DHCPNAK            _____
```

This lab demonstrated how to configure the Catalyst 4006 L3 Services Module as a DHCP relay agent, allowing hosts downstream to acquire dynamically allocated IP addresses.

Lab 8-1: Hot Standby Router Protocol

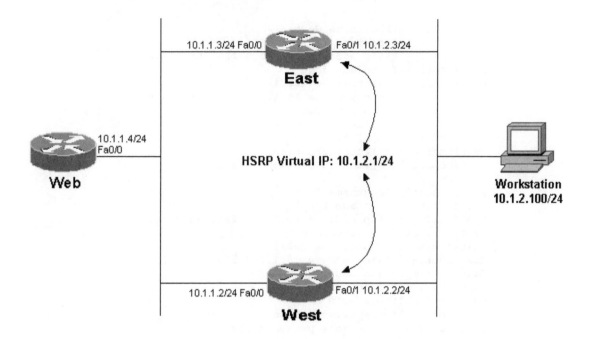

Objective

Configure Hot Standby Router Protocol (HSRP) on a pair of routers to provide redundant router services to a network.

Scenario

Two routers are connected to your network. Using two default gateways does not provide a reliable path in the event of an outage. Configuring HSRP on your two routers provides a fast failover mechanism that is transparent to the users. This allows hosts on the LAN segment to maintain access to the web router in the event of a router failure.

Step 1

Cable the lab as shown in the diagram.

Step 2

Configure the web router to act as a web server. Configure the router with a username/password, and enable HTTP management services:

```
Router(config)#hostname Web
Web(config)#interface fa0/0
Web(config-if)#ip address 10.1.1.4 255.255.255.0
Web(config-if)#no shutdown
Web(config-if)#line vty 0 4
Web(config-line)#login
Web(config-line)#password cisco
Web(config-line)#enable password class
Web(config)#ip http server
```

Step 3

Configure the East and West routers:

```
Router(config)#hostname West
West(config)#interface fa0/0
West(config-if)#ip address 10.1.1.2 255.255.255.0
West(config-if)#no shutdown
West(config-if)#interface fa0/1
West(config-if)#ip address 10.1.2.2 255.255.255.0
West(config-if)#no shutdown
West(config-if)#line vty 0 4
West(config-line)#login
West(config-line)#password cisco
West(config-line)#enable password class

Router(config)#hostname East
East(config)#interface fa0/0
East(config-if)#ip address 10.1.1.3 255.255.255.0
East(config-if)#no shutdown
East(config-if)#interface fa0/1
East(config-if)#ip address 10.1.2.3 255.255.255.0
East(config-if)#no shutdown
East(config-if)#line vty 0 4
East(config-line)#login
East(config-line)#password cisco
East(config-line)#enable password class
```

Step 4

Configure EIGRP on all routers:

```
Web(config)#router eigrp 10
Web(config-router)#network 10.0.0.0

West(config)#router eigrp 10
West(config-router)#network 10.0.0.0

East(config)#router eigrp 10
East(config-router)#network 10.0.0.0
```

Specify the default gateway for the workstation. Because two routers are present on each network, you specify both routers as candidate default routers.

On the workstation:

Configure your workstation with the IP address 10.1.2.100/24. Use the two default gateways: 10.1.2.2 and 10.1.2.3.

Step 5

You should now be able to ping the web server, 10.1.1.4, from your workstation.

1. Can you ping successfully? _____

If not, troubleshoot your configurations to determine where the problem is.

Step 6

As soon as you can successfully ping the web server/router, unplug the cable connected to interface Fa0/1 on the West router.

2. Now try to ping again. What happens?

_____
_____
_____

3. Why is this happening?

_____
_____

Plug your cable back into the West router.

Wait a few seconds. It might take some time for the Ethernet ports to reach the STP Forwarding state if you do not have PortFast configured (assuming that you are not using a hub to connect the devices).

4. Try your ping again. Does it work now? _____

Step 7

HSRP dramatically improves this situation.

You currently have two IP addresses on each network used by the routers—one IP address for each router. HSRP lets you create a third virtual IP address that "floats" between the routers, in the event that one of the routers fails. You use the 10.1.2.1 address on each of the networks for the HSRP address.

You turn on HSRP using the **standby ip** command at the interface level. You make West the active HSRP router by setting the priority to 110. (The default is 100.) You use the **preempt** keyword to allow the router with the highest priority (West) to take over as the active HSRP router (even if East is currently the active HSRP router; this is the situation when West's interface Fa0/1 goes down and then comes back up).

Turn on HSRP on the 10.1.2.0 network:

```
West(config)#interface fa0/1
West(config-if)#standby ip 10.1.2.1
West(config-if)#standby priority 110 preempt

East(config)#interface fa0/1
East(config-if)#standby ip 10.1.2.1
East(config-if)#standby preempt
```

Step 8

Reconfigure your workstation: Remove the current default gateways, and install just a single default gateway pointing to the HSRP virtual IP address of 10.1.2.1/24.

Step 9

Try to ping the web router at 10.1.1.4.

5. Can you ping? _____

If you can't ping, go back and troubleshoot your configuration.

Step 10

Remove the cable from interface Fa0/1 on the West router again.

6. Try your ping again. Does it work now? _____

Step 11

Do a **show standby** command:

```
West#show standby
FastEthernet0/1 - Group 0
  Local state is Standby, priority 110
  Hellotime 3 holdtime 10
  Next hello sent in 00:00:01.542
  Hot standby IP address is 10.1.2.1 configured
  Active router is 10.1.2.3 expires in 00:00:08
  Standby router is local
  Standby virtual mac address is 0000.0c07.ac00
```

7. Notice that HSRP creates a standby virtual MAC address. Why does it need a standby virtual MAC address?

_____

_____

Try the **show standby** command on the East router.

Replug the cable into interface Fa0/1 on the West router. Try your ping again. Then enter the **show standby** command again on the West router.

This lab demonstrated the basic configuration of HSRP. HSRP provides fast failover for devices on a LAN segment containing two or more Cisco routers.

Lab 9-1: IP/TV Software Installation

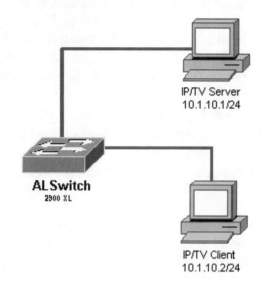

IP/TV Server
10.1.10.1/24

AL Switch
2900 XL

IP/TV Client
10.1.10.2/24

Objective

Install the IP/TV software.

Scenario

You must configure the Cisco IP/TV Multicast Server and Viewer for multicast lab testing.

Note: An IP/TV Demo CD is available at www.cisco.com (search for **IP/TV Demo** or go directly to www.cisco.com/warp/public/cc/pd/mxsv/iptv3400/index.shtml). If you decide to use other multicast software, be sure that it delivers streaming video via multicast streams and not via unicast UDP streams.

Step 1

Cable the lab as shown in the diagram.

Step 2

Clear the NVRAM on the Cisco 2900 XL and reload. There will be no added configurations to the 2900 XL switch after you clear the NVRAM and reload.

Step 3

Configure both the Client Viewer and Multicast Server systems. The machines for both clients and servers can be Windows 95, 98, NT, or 2000 300 MHz or larger systems with 64 MB or more of RAM and 450 MB or more of free disk space. Ensure that the IP addresses are set as indicated in the diagram. Make sure that the systems can ping each other before you continue.

For your reference, we used the following operating systems and browsers to successfully complete the labs in this chapter:

- **IP/TV Client**—Windows 98 Second Edition with Internet Explorer 5.5 and IP/TV Viewer 3.0.662.0
- **IP/TV Server**—Windows 2000 Server with Internet Explorer 5.0 and IP/TV Server 3.0.662.0
- **2900 XL Switch**—Cisco IOS Software Release 12.0(5)XU
- **2621 Router**—Cisco IOS Software Release 12.0(5)T1
- **4006 Supervisor Engine II**—CatOS 7.2(2)
- **4006 L3 Module**—Cisco IOS Software Release 12.0(10)W5(18f)

Step 4

You install the IP/TV software on both the server and the client. The IP/TV Demo CD jacket contains an installation and requirements document that you should follow. Ensure that your systems meet the necessary requirements for the role of server or viewer.

A. To install the IP/TV server software, follow these steps:

1. Insert the IP/TV Demo CD into the Microsoft Windows computer located at 10.1.10.1. An installation screen should appear. If it does not, double-click the CD icon from My Computer.

2. Select to install the demo server, as indicated in the following figure.

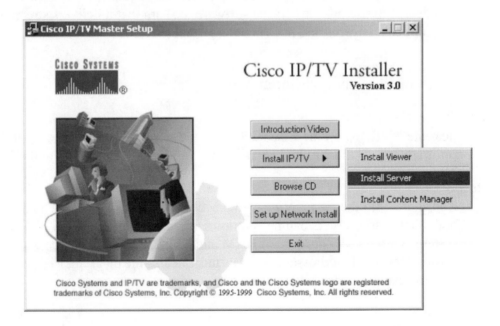

3. Select the defaults until you see the following screen. Use the information provided next to fill in the blanks. Be sure to enter **Demo** for the serial number if you're using the IP/TV Demo CD.

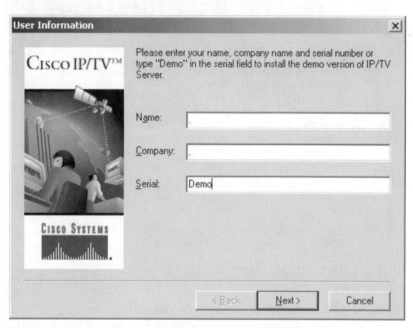

4. Select the defaults until the following screen appears. Note that it often takes 15 minutes or so to reach this screen. After you click **Finish**, your system reboots, and the installation is complete.

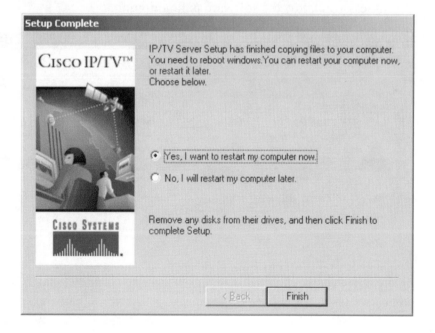

148

5. Start the IP/TV software. Double-click the **IP/TV Server** icon on your desktop to start the program. It should look like the following figure.

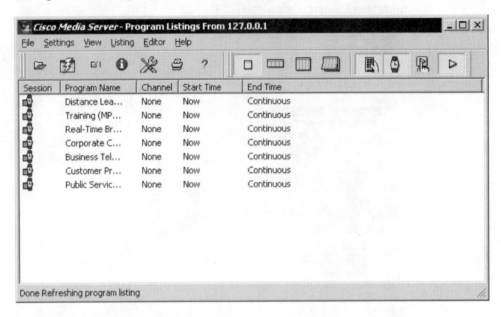

6. Enable the continuous streams of video that are used for testing. Right-click the stream **Corporate Communications**, and select **Enable/Disable Program**, as shown in the following figure. This starts the multicast stream to all devices connected to ALSwitch. You will install a client on ALSwitch to verify the IP/TV operation. It does not make sense to continue unless you know the software is functioning.

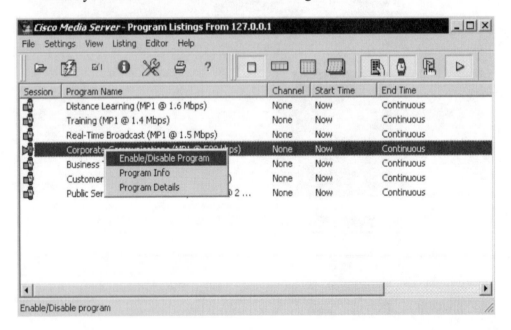

7. Verify the multicast address of the current streamed process. Right-click the current stream and select **Properties**. You should see something similar to the following figure, with possibly different multicast addresses.

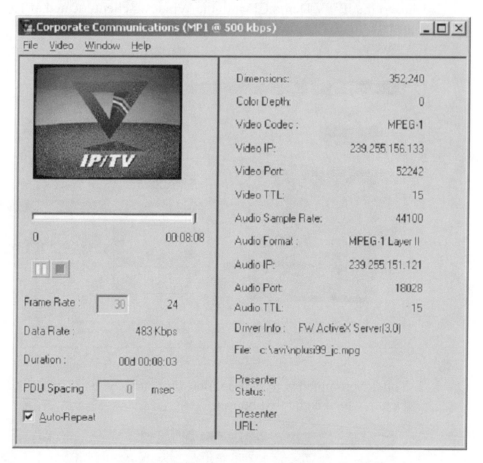

1. What are your multicast addresses? _____

B. To install the IP/TV Viewer client software, complete the following steps. Remember that you should install the client software on 10.1.10.2 because it is in the same broadcast domain as the server. Recall that 10.1.10.1 is the IP address of the IP/TV server:

1. Insert the IP/TV Demo CD into the Windows client located at 10.1.10.2. An installation screen should appear. Select the option shown here to install the viewer.

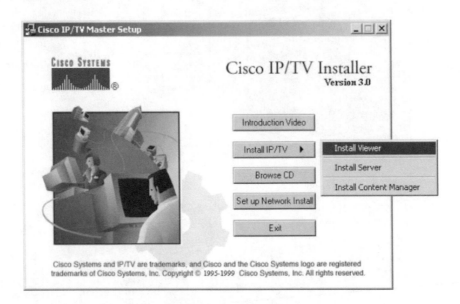

2. You are prompted with two options. Of course, you are installing the Demo, which is the first button.

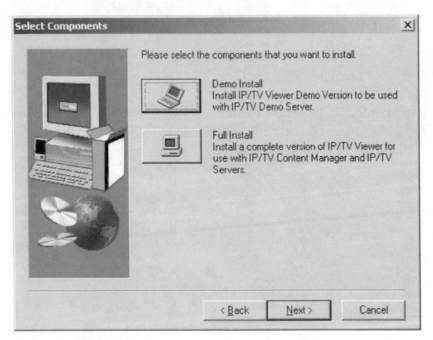

3. Enter **Client**, as shown in the following figure, and click **Next**. Continue accepting the defaults until the installation is complete. You are prompted to reboot, so go ahead and do so at that time.

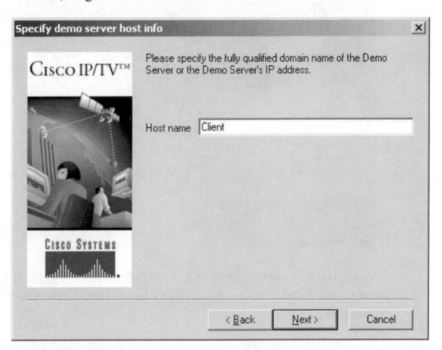

4. Click the **IP/TV Viewer** icon on your desktop when the system reboots. You see the following screen.

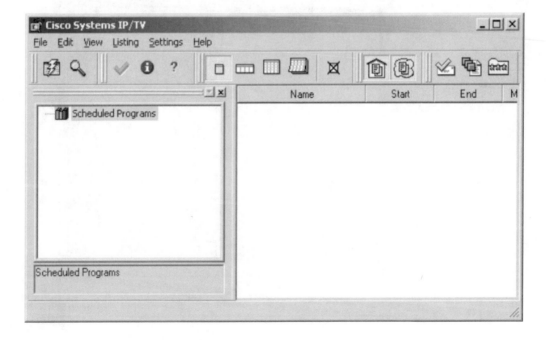

5. You need to identify the IP/TV servers you want to use. As shown in the following figure, select **Settings, Content Managers**.

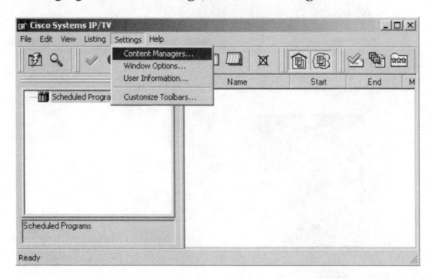

6. You see the following dialog box. Highlight **Client** and click **Remove** because the local host is not necessary here. Then click **Add Content Manager**.

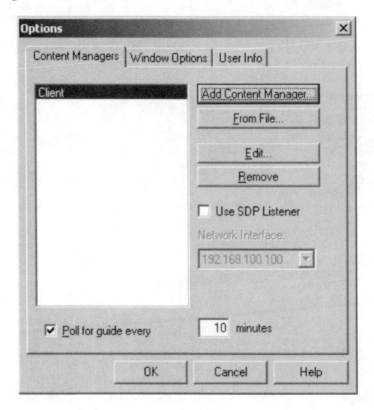

7. Add the Content Manager, as shown next. Pay close attention to the port you enter. It is 8080 for the IP/TV server instead of the default of 80.

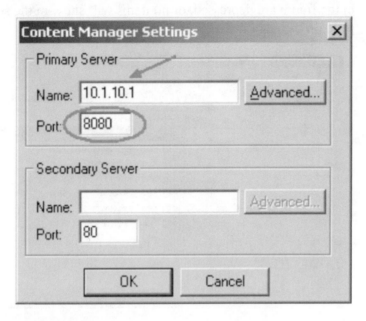

8. Your screen should appear as follows because 10.1.10.1 is your IP/TV multicast server. Click **OK**.

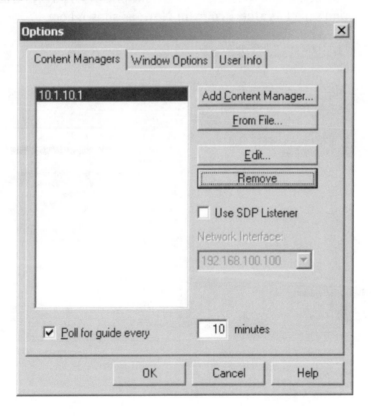

9. Your listings should refresh automatically. If they don't, you can click the lightning bolt on the toolbar to refresh. Ensure that the circled items shown in the figure are depressed, or no items will show in the scheduled programs pane on the right.

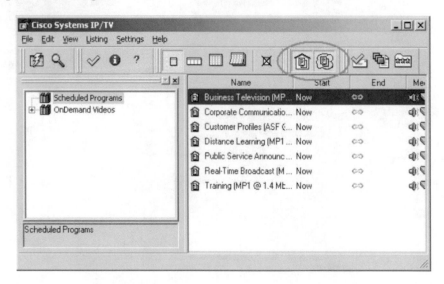

10. This completes the installation. Let's view the continuous stream you enabled on the IP/TV server. Right-click **Corporate Communications** and select **Watch Program Now**, as shown here.

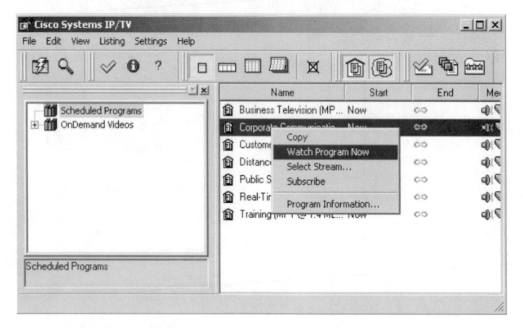

11. You should see the following screen. It indicates that your network is successfully propagating multicast traffic.

This lab demonstrated the installation of the Cisco IP/TV Server and Client with the Demo CD. This software will be used for the subsequent multicast routing labs.

Lab 9-2: Multicast Routing with Protocol-Independent Multicast Dense Mode

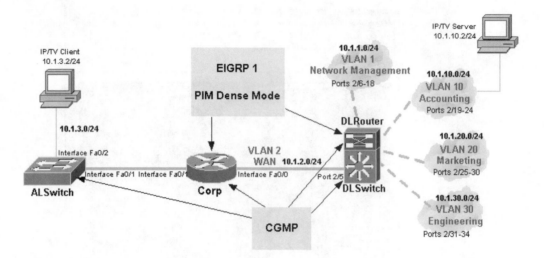

Objective

Configure multicast routing on the Catalyst 4006 L3 module using Protocol-Independent Multicast Dense Mode (PIM-DM).

Scenario

Current Environment

Your network switching equipment currently includes a 4006 switch, a 2900 XL access switch, and a Cisco 2600 series access router. Your network is segmented into four functional VLANs for better network management. These VLANs include Accounting, Marketing, and Engineering, for the users and the default native VLAN for network management. Inter-VLAN routing has been implemented using an L3 module on the 4006 to allow individuals and servers on your VLANs to exchange information.

Enhancement

Your LAN functions well. Your company's executives decided to implement an IP/TV multicast system throughout the LAN to include the access switch connected to the external access WAN router (as illustrated in the diagram). The implementation calls for the IP/TV server to be connected to VLAN 10 and clients to be connected to any Ethernet segment on the corporate LAN, including the external access router, as illustrated in the diagram. PIM-DM has been selected as the multicast routing protocol for corporate LAN multicast traffic.

Design

VTP configuration:

Switch	VTP Domain	VTP Mode	VTP Pruning
DLSwitch	Corp	Server	Enabled
ALSwitch	—	—	—

VLAN configuration:

VLAN ID	VLAN Name	VLAN Subnet	VLAN Gateway
1	Default (native)	10.1.1.0/24	10.1.1.1
2	WAN	10.1.2.0/24	10.1.2.1
10	Accounting	10.1.10.0/24	10.1.10.1
20	Marketing	10.1.20.0/24	10.1.20.1
30	Engineering	10.1.30.0/24	10.1.30.1

Other LAN configuration:

Network	Description	Subnet	Gateway
3	External	10.1.3.0/24	10.1.3.1

Switch VLAN port/interface assignments:

Switch	VLAN 1	VLAN 2	VLAN 10	VLAN 20	VLAN 30
DLSwitch	6–18	5	19–24	25–30	31–34
ALSwitch	All	—	—	—	—

Catalyst 4006 DLRouter interface configuration:

Interface	IP Address	VLAN
PortChannel 1	10.1.1.1/24	Native 1
PortChannel 1.2	10.1.2.1/24	2
PortChannel 1.10	10.1.10.1/24	10
PortChannel 1.20	10.1.20.1/24	20
PortChannel 1.30	10.1.30.1/24	30

Cisco 2600 Internet router interface configuration:

Interface	IP Address
FastEthernet 0/0	10.1.2.2/24
FastEthernet 0/1	10.1.3.1/24

Routing protocols:

Description	Protocol	ID
LAN/WAN	EIGRP	1
Multicast	PIM-DM	—

Notes

_____

_____

_____

_____

_____

_____

_____

_____

_____

_____

_____

_____

_____

_____

Step 1

Cable the lab as shown in the diagram. We will not explain the steps for basic LAN configuration because this lab focuses on multicasting. Also, this lab requires that you have already performed the IP/TV installation and configuration lab and that both the server and viewer are available for use.

Step 2

The first device to be configured is the distribution layer switch, DLSwitch. Access the switch through the console port and enter privileged mode. Clear your NVRAM and reload:

```
Console> (enable) clear config all
Console> (enable) reset
```

After the switch resets, enter privileged mode and issue the command **show config**. Simply review the default configuration. It is useful to be aware of "clean" configuration settings.

Step 3

Configure DLSwitch with the following information.

a. Configure the prompt on the 4006 switch:

```
Console> (enable) set system name DLSwitch
```

Note: Verify using **show config**.

b. Configure VTP information on the 4006 switch:

```
DLSwitch> (enable) set vtp domain Corp
DLSwitch> (enable) set vtp mode server
```

Note: Verify using **show vtp domain**.

c. Create corporate VLANs:

```
DLSwitch> (enable) set vlan 2 name WAN
DLSwitch> (enable) set vlan 10 name Accounting
DLSwitch> (enable) set vlan 20 name Marketing
DLSwitch> (enable) set vlan 30 name Engineering
```

Note: Verify using **show vlan**.

d. Set port channel admin groups:

```
DLSwitch> (enable) set port channel 2/1-2 156
```

Note: Verify using **show config**.

e. Assign port VLAN memberships:

```
DLSwitch> (enable) set vlan 2     2/5
DLSwitch> (enable) set vlan 10    2/19-24
DLSwitch> (enable) set vlan 20    2/25-30
DLSwitch> (enable) set vlan 30    2/31-34
```

Note: Verify using **show vlan**. You see that all VLANs default to VLAN 1.

f. Establish VLAN trunking:

```
DLSwitch> (enable) set trunk 2/1 nonegotiate dot1q 1-1005
DLSwitch> (enable) set trunk 2/2 nonegotiate dot1q 1-1005
```

Note: The **show trunk** command might not display active trunking because the trunk links might not yet be active.

g. Establish Fast EtherChannel on trunking interfaces:

```
DLSwitch> (enable) set port channel 2/1-2 mode on
```

Note: Verify using **show channel**.

h. Enable the spanning tree PortFast option for the port on the 4006 switch connecting to the external router:

```
DLSwitch> (enable) set spantree portfast 2/5 enable
```

i. Enable Cisco Group Management Protocol (CGMP) on the switch. CGMP lets the switch communicate with directly connected routers to eliminate extraneous multicast traffic.

```
DLSwitch> (enable) set cgmp enable
```

j. You'll also enable CGMP leave processing. This feature speeds up the process of a multicast client's switch port curtailing the transmission of multicast traffic after the client has indicated it is no longer interested in receiving the traffic. (A client indicates this by sending an IGMPv2 leave message.)

```
DLSwitch> (enable) set cgmp leave enable
```

k. Verify the complete configuration using **show config**.

Step 4

Configure DLRouter with the following information.

a. Configure the host name, DLRouter, on the 4006 L3 module:

```
Router(config)#hostname DLRouter
```

Note: Verify using **show run**.

b. Configure DLRouter on the 4006 L3 module for multicast routing:

```
Router(config)#ip multicast-routing
```

Note: Verify using **show run**.

c. Configure the VLAN interface addressing and trunking information. Configure PIM-DM and CGMP on the port channel interface and its subinterfaces:

```
DLRouter (config)#interface Port-channel1
DLRouter (config-if)#ip address 10.1.1.1 255.255.255.0
DLRouter (config-if)#no shutdown

DLRouter (config)#interface Port-channel1.2
DLRouter (config-if)#encapsulation dot1Q 2
DLRouter (config-if)#ip address 10.1.2.1 255.255.255.0
DLRouter (config-if)#ip pim dense-mode
DLRouter (config-if)#ip cgmp

DLRouter (config)#interface Port-channel1.10
DLRouter (config-if)#encapsulation dot1Q 10
DLRouter (config-if)#ip address 10.1.10.1 255.255.255.0
DLRouter (config-if)#ip pim dense-mode
DLRouter (config-if)#ip cgmp

DLRouter (config)#interface Port-channel1.20
DLRouter (config-if)#encapsulation dot1Q 20
DLRouter (config-if)#ip address 10.1.20.1 255.255.255.0
DLRouter (config-if)#ip pim dense-mode
DLRouter (config-if)#ip cgmp
```

```
DLRouter (config)#interface Port-channel1.30
DLRouter (config-if)#encapsulation dot1Q 30
DLRouter (config-if)#ip address 10.1.30.1 255.255.255.0
DLRouter (config-if)#ip pim dense-mode
DLRouter (config-if)#ip cgmp
```

Note: Verify using **show run**.

d. Assign the gigabit interfaces to the port channel. This is required for the VLANs to establish communication with the switch.

```
DLRouter (config)#interface GigabitEthernet3
DLRouter (config-if)#channel-group 1

DLRouter (config)#interface GigabitEthernet4
DLRouter (config-if)#channel-group 1
```

Note: Verify using **show run**.

e. Configure the corporate routing protocol. The PIM routing protocol used for Dense or Sparse Mode relies on routes discovered by an interior gateway routing protocol. In this lab, you use EIGRP. You advertise the entire 10.x.x.x network to cover all subnetworks.

```
DLRouter (config)#router eigrp 1
DLRouter (config-router)#network 10.0.0.0
```

f. Verify the complete configuration using **show run**.

Step 5

Configure Corp with the following information.

a. Configure the host name, Corp, on the external 2600:

```
Router(config)#hostname Corp
```

Note: Verify using **show run**.

b. Enable IP multicast routing on Corp:

```
Corp(config)#ip multicast-routing
```

Note: Verify using **show run**.

c. Configure each interface for the PIM-DM multicast routing protocol. Configure CGMP on the ALSwitch-connected interface to eliminate extraneous multicast traffic forwarded by ALSwitch to its directly connected multicast clients:

```
Corp (config)#interface FastEthernet0/0
Corp (config-if)#ip address 10.1.2.2 255.255.255.0
Corp (config-if)#ip pim dense-mode
Corp (config-if)#ip cgmp
```

```
Corp (config)#interface FastEthernet0/1
Corp (config-if)#ip address 10.1.3.1 255.255.255.0
Corp (config-if)#ip pim dense-mode
Corp (config-if)#ip cgmp
```

Note: Verify using **show run**.

    d. Configure EIGRP on the 2600. PIM-DM multicast routing depends on EIGRP discovered routes for this scenario.

```
Router (config)#router eigrp 1
Router (config-router)#network 10.0.0.0
```

Note: Verify using **show run**.

Step 6

Configure ALSwitch with the following information.

    a. Clear your NVRAM and reset the switch for a clean configuration:

```
Switch#erase start
Switch#reload
```

Note: If asked to save your system configuration, enter **n** for no.

    b. Configure the host name, ALSwitch, on the external 2900:

```
Switch(config)#hostname ALSwitch
```

Note: Verify using **show run**.

    c. Configure CGMP leave processing on the 2900 XL:

```
ALSwitch (config)#cgmp leave-processing
```

Note: Verify using **show run**.

Step 7

Configure, connect, and test IP multicast devices and software.

    a. Connect the IP/TV multicast server to any VLAN 10 port on the 4006 switch (ports 2/19–24). Ensure that the IP address of the multicast server is 10.1.10.2/24 with a gateway of 10.1.10.1.

Use the **ipconfig** or **winipcfg** command from the DOS prompt (depending on your version of Microsoft operating system) to verify your entries.

    b. From a *command prompt on the multicast server,* use the **ping** command to test your ability to reach the gateway IP address, 10.1.10.1, and the external network gateway, 10.1.3.1:

```
C:\>ping 10.1.10.1
```

```
C:\>ping 10.1.3.1
```

Note: If these **ping** commands do not function, you need to troubleshoot the problem before continuing.

c. On the IP/TV multicast server, activate the IP/TV media server software. Right-click the multicast stream **Corporate Communications** and select **Enable/Disable Program**, as shown in the following figure. Ensure that the green activation indicator is displayed on the software management screen.

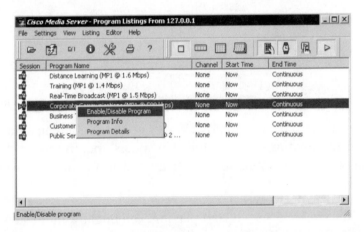

d. Connect the IP/TV *multicast client* PC to interface Fa0/2 on ALSwitch. Because you are not trunking to ALSwitch, all ports should represent the same subnet that is isolated to that switch. Ensure that the client PC's IP address is set to 10.1.3.2/24 with a gateway of 10.1.3.1.

Use the **ipconfig** or **winipcfg** command from the DOS prompt to verify your entries.

e. From a *command prompt on the multicast client,* use the **ping** command to test connectivity to the multicast server IP address 10.1.10.2:

```
C:\>ping 10.1.10.2
```

Note: If these **ping** commands do not function, you need to troubleshoot the problem before continuing.

f. On the IP/TV multicast client, activate the IP/TV viewer software. Ensure that the Content Manager settings are configured as shown in the following figure. Be sure to change the port and IP addresses as indicated.

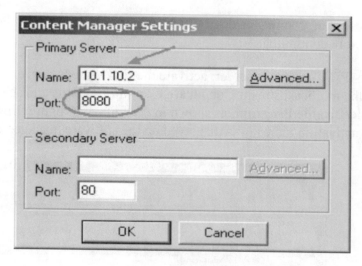

g. Refresh the screen on the IP/TV viewer and double-click the **Corporate Communications** stream. John Chambers' speech should start streaming from the server. Congratulations. You are now using multicast routing with PIM-DM.

Note: If the stream does not start playing, you might want to stop and then restart the stream from the IP/TV server. If it still does not start, there is a problem. Use the next section to help in your troubleshooting because multicast routing is generally difficult to troubleshoot. In any case, complete the remainder of the lab.

Step 8

Investigate and troubleshoot multicast processing. Note that you should activate the stream on the client before executing these commands. This gives you the full effect of the troubleshooting information.

a. Show the content addressable memory (CAM) entries on DLSwitch. The CAM table on the switch contains a mapping of Ethernet addresses to ports that the switch uses to forward traffic. A port can have multiple mappings. CGMP permits dynamic updates of this table for multicast entries.

```
DLSwitch> (enable) show cam dynamic
```

1. How many CAM entries are in your table? _____

b. Show the CGMP statistics. This command displays CGMP activity information. Then complete the following table:

```
DLSwitch> (enable) show cgmp statistics

CGMP enabled

CGMP statistics for vlan 1:
valid rx pkts received          _____
invalid rx pkts received        _____
```

```
                valid cgmp joins received        _____
                valid cgmp leaves received       _____
                valid igmp leaves received       _____
                valid igmp queries received      _____
                igmp gs queries transmitted      _____
                igmp leaves transmitted          _____
                failures to add GDA to EARL      _____
                topology notifications received  _____

   DLSwitch> (enable) show cgmp statistics 2

   CGMP enabled

   CGMP statistics for vlan 2:
                valid rx pkts received           _____
                invalid rx pkts received         _____
                valid cgmp joins received        _____
                valid cgmp leaves received       _____
                valid igmp leaves received       _____
                valid igmp queries received      _____
                igmp gs queries transmitted      _____
                igmp leaves transmitted          _____
                failures to add GDA to EARL      _____
                topology notifications received  _____
```

c. Let's explore your PIM information on DLRouter. Recall that you are using PIM-DM. Complete the following tables:

```
   DLRouter#show ip pim neighbor

   PIM Neighbor Table
   Neighbor Address   Interface          Uptime     Expires   Ver  Mode
                                          00:10:18   00:01:18  v2
   _____         _____                                _____

   DLRouter#show ip pim neighbor interface

   Address       Interface          Version/Mode   Nbr   Query    DR
                                                         Count    Intvl
   _____      Port-channel____   _____   0     30       _____
   _____      Port-channel____   _____   0     30       _____
   _____      Port-channel____   _____   0     30       _____
   _____      Port-channel____   _____   0     30       _____
   _____      Port-channel____   _____   0     30       _____

   DLRouter#show ip pim interface count
```

2. How many multicast packets have been sent and received on each interface?

_____

```
   DLRouter#debug ip pim
```

3. What router is sending PIM reports to DLRouter? _____

The following command is useful for monitoring multicast group memberships:

```
   DLRouter#show ip igmp group
```

4. Which two streams are identified in the group memberships?

_____

d. Let's explore the PIM information on Corp. Most of the commands have sample output. Your numbers might not match. These commands are useful troubleshooting tools.

```
Corp#show ip pim neighbor
```

5. From the table, who are your PIM neighbors?

_____

```
Corp#show ip pim neighbor interface

Address     Interface         Version/Mode   Nbr   Query   DR
                                                   Count   Intvl
10.1.2.2    FastEthernet0/0   v2/Dense        1    30      10.1.2.2
10.1.3.1    FastEthernet0/1   v2/Dense        0    30      10.1.3.1

Corp#show ip pim interface count

State: * - Fast Switched, D - Distributed Fast Switched
       H - Hardware Switched
Address            Interface         FS   Mpackets In/Out
10.1.2.2           FastEthernet0/0    *    46539/231
10.1.3.1           FastEthernet0/1    *    231/41443

Corp#show ip igmp groups

IGMP Connected Group Membership
Group Address     Interface         Uptime     Expires   Last Reporter
239.255.156.133   FastEthernet0/1   00:10:20   00:02:40  10.1.3.2
224.0.1.40        FastEthernet0/1   00:17:00   never     10.1.3.1
239.255.151.121   FastEthernet0/1   00:10:20   00:02:36  10.1.3.2

Corp#debug ip cgmp

CGMP debugging is on

Corp#debug ip igmp

IGMP debugging is on

00:18:01: IGMP: Send v2 Query on FastEthernet0/1 to 224.0.0.1
00:18:01: IGMP: Set report delay time to 8.8 seconds for 224.0.1.40 on
00:18:06: IGMP: Received v2 Report from 10.1.3.2 (FastEthernet0/1) for 239.255.151.121
00:18:06: IGMP: Received v2 Report from 10.1.3.2 (FastEthernet0/1) for 239.255.156.133
00:18:10: IGMP: Send v2 Report for 224.0.1.40 on FastEthernet0/1
00:18:10: IGMP: Received v2 Report from 10.1.3.1 (FastEthernet0/1) for 224.0.1.40
```

e. Show the multicast routing table on DLRouter and Corp. Viewing the multicast routing table is the primary tool for troubleshooting multicast routing. The output displays several items, including routing, PIM, and stream information:

```
DLRouter#show ip mroute
```

6. Can you identify the multicast streams?

_____

The following command is the most useful tool for troubleshooting IP multicast routing:

```
Corp#show ip mroute
```

7. Can you identify the multicast streams?

_____

f. Repeat the last step, but first unplug the multicast server:

```
DLRouter#show ip mroute

Corp#show ip mroute
```

8. Can you identify any multicast streams?

_____

_____

This lab demonstrated how to configure PIM-DM for use with a multicast server and multicast clients in a campus LAN.

Lab 9-3: Multicast Routing with Protocol-Independent Multicast Sparse Mode

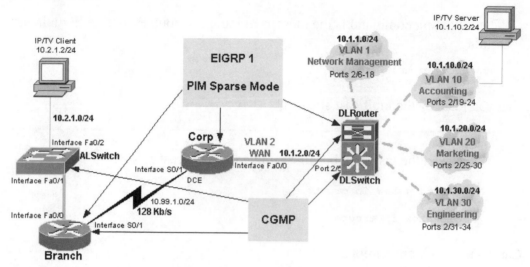

Objective

Configure multicast routing on the Catalyst 4006 L3 Services Module using Protocol-Independent Multicast Sparse Mode (PIM-SM).

Scenario

Current Environment

Your corporate network equipment currently includes a 4006 switch with an L3 module for VLAN routing and a Cisco 2600 external access router. Your corporate network is segmented into four functional VLANs for better network management. These VLANs include Accounting, Marketing, and Engineering for the users and the default native VLAN for network management. Inter-VLAN routing has been implemented using the L3 Services module. No VLAN trunking to the external router has been configured. Connected to your corporate network via a 128 Kbps leased line is your branch network, which includes a 2600 Cisco WAN router and a 2900 XL switch for local access.

Enhancement

Your LAN and WAN connections function well. Your company's executives decided to implement an IP/TV multicast system throughout the LAN to include the access switch connected to the branch router over the WAN. The branch LAN facilitate only audio streams to reduce WAN congestion, until a faster WAN connection can be leased or purchased. The implementation calls for the IP/TV server to be connected to VLAN 10 and for clients to be connected to any Ethernet segment on the corporate LAN and branch office LAN, as illustrated in the diagram. PIM-SM has been selected as the multicast routing protocol for corporate WAN multicast traffic. The corporate 2600 router has been selected as the PIM-SM Rendezvous Point (RP).

Design

VTP configuration:

Switch	VTP Domain	VTP Mode	VTP Pruning
DLSwitch	Corp	Server	Enabled
ALSwitch	—	—	—

VLAN configuration:

VLAN ID	VLAN Name	VLAN Subnet	VLAN Gateway
1	Default (native)	10.1.1.0/24	10.1.1.1
2	WAN	10.1.2.0/24	10.1.2.1
10	Accounting	10.1.10.0/24	10.1.10.1
20	Marketing	10.1.20.0/24	10.1.20.1
30	Engineering	10.1.30.0/24	10.1.30.1

Other LAN/WAN configuration:

Network	Description	Subnet	Gateway
Branch	Remote/LAN	10.2.1.0/24	10.2.1.1
WAN	Remote/WAN	10.99.1.0/24	—

VLAN port/interface assignments:

Switch	VLAN 1	VLAN 2	VLAN 10	VLAN 20	VLAN 30
DLSwitch	6–18	5	19–24	25–30	31–34
ALSwitch	All	—	—	—	—

Catalyst 4006 DLRouter interface configuration:

Interface	IP Address	VLAN
PortChannel 1	10.1.1.1/24	Native 1
PortChannel 1.2	10.1.2.1/24	2
PortChannel 1.10	10.1.10.1/24	10
PortChannel 1.20	10.1.20.1/24	20
PortChannel 1.30	10.1.30.1/24	30

Cisco 2600 WAN router interface configuration:

Interface	IP Address	Location
Serial 0/1 (DCE)	10.99.1.1	Corp
Serial 0/1	10.99.1.2	Branch
FastEthernet 0/0	10.1.2.2/24	Corp
FastEthernet 0/0	10.2.1.1/24	Branch

Routing protocols:

Description	Protocol	ID
LAN/WAN	EIGRP	1
Multicast	PIM-SM	RP=10.99.1.1

Notes

_____
_____
_____
_____
_____
_____
_____
_____
_____
_____
_____
_____

Step 1

Cable the lab as shown in the diagram. We will not explain the steps for basic LAN configuration because this lab focuses on multicasting. Also, this lab requires that you have already performed Lab 9-1 and that both the server and viewer are available for use.

Step 2

The first device to be configured is be the distribution layer switch DLSwitch. Access the switch through the console port and enter privileged mode. Clear your NVRAM and reload:

```
Console> (enable) clear config all
Console> (enable) reset
```

After the switch resets, enter privileged mode and issue the command **show config**. Simply review the default configuration. It is useful to be aware of "clean" configuration settings.

Step 3

Configure DLSwitch with the following information.

    a. Configure the system name on the 4006 switch.

Note: Verify using **show config**.

    b. Configure VTP information on the 4006 switch:

```
DLSwitch> (enable) set vtp domain Corp
DLSwitch> (enable) set vtp mode server
```

Note: Verify using **show vtp domain**.

    c. Create corporate VLANs:

```
DLSwitch> (enable) set vlan 2 name WAN
DLSwitch> (enable) set vlan 10 name Accounting
DLSwitch> (enable) set vlan 20 name Marketing
DLSwitch> (enable) set vlan 30 name Engineering
```

Note: Verify using **show vlan**.

    d. Set port channel admin groups:

```
DLSwitch> (enable) set port channel 2/1-2 156
```

Note: Verify using **show config**.

    e. Assign port VLAN memberships:

```
DLSwitch> (enable) set vlan 2     2/5
DLSwitch> (enable) set vlan 10    2/19-24
DLSwitch> (enable) set vlan 20    2/25-30
DLSwitch> (enable) set vlan 30    2/31-34
```

Note: Verify using **show vlan**. If you use the **show vlan** command, you see that all VLANs default to VLAN 1.

    f. Establish VLAN trunking:

```
DLSwitch> (enable) set trunk 2/1 nonegotiate dot1q 1-1005
DLSwitch> (enable) set trunk 2/2 nonegotiate dot1q 1-1005
```

Note: The **show trunk** command might not display active trunking because the trunk links might not yet be active.

    g. Establish Fast EtherChannel on trunking interfaces:

```
DLSwitch> (enable) set port channel 2/1-2 mode on
```

Note: Verify using **show channel**.

h. Enable the spanning tree PortFast option for the port on the 4006 switch connecting to the external router:

```
DLSwitch> (enable) set spantree portfast 2/5 enable
```

i. Enable CGMP on the switch. CGMP lets the switch communicate with directly connected routers to eliminate extraneous multicast traffic:

```
DLSwitch> (enable) set cgmp enable
```

j. You'll also enable CGMP leave processing. This feature speeds up the process of a multicast client's switch port curtailing the transmission of multicast traffic after the client has indicated it is no longer interested in receiving the traffic. (A client indicates this by sending an IGMPv2 leave message.)

```
DLSwitch> (enable) set cgmp leave enable
```

k. Verify the complete configuration using **show config**.

Step 4

Configure DLRouter with the following information.

a. Configure the host name, DLRouter, on the 4006 L3 module:

```
Router(config)#hostname DLRouter
```

Note: Verify using **show run**.

b. Configure DLRouter on the 4006 L3 module for multicast routing:

```
Router(config)#ip multicast-routing
```

Note: Verify using **show run**.

c. Configure the VLAN interface addressing and trunking information. Note that on subinterface 1.2, you could have used PIM Sparse-Dense Mode. This would allow the external router to run either PIM Sparse or Dense Mode, depending on the availability of an RP:

```
DLRouter(config)#interface Port-channel1
DLRouter(config-if)#ip address 10.1.1.1 255.255.255.0
DLRouter(config-if)#no shutdown

DLRouter(config)#interface Port-channel1.2
DLRouter(config-if)#encapsulation dot1Q 2
DLRouter(config-if)#ip address 10.1.2.1 255.255.255.0
DLRouter(config-if)#ip pim sparse-mode
DLRouter(config-if)#ip cgmp

DLRouter(config)#interface Port-channel1.10
DLRouter(config-if)#encapsulation dot1Q 10
DLRouter(config-if)#ip address 10.1.10.1 255.255.255.0
DLRouter(config-if)#ip pim sparse-mode
DLRouter(config-if)#ip cgmp
```

```
DLRouter(config)#interface Port-channel1.20
DLRouter(config-if)#encapsulation dot1Q 20
DLRouter(config-if)#ip address 10.1.20.1 255.255.255.0
DLRouter(config-if)#ip pim sparse-mode
DLRouter(config-if)#ip cgmp

DLRouter(config)#interface Port-channel1.30
DLRouter(config-if)#encapsulation dot1Q 30
DLRouter(config-if)#ip address 10.1.30.1 255.255.255.0
DLRouter(config-if)#ip pim sparse-mode
DLRouter(config-if)#ip cgmp
```

Note: Verify using **show run**.

d. Assign the gigabit interfaces to the port channel. This is required for the VLANs to establish communication with the switch:

```
DLRouter (config)#interface GigabitEthernet3
DLRouter (config-if)#channel-group 1

DLRouter (config)#interface GigabitEthernet4
DLRouter (config-if)#channel-group 1
```

Note: Verify using **show run**.

e. Configure the corporate routing protocol. The PIM routing protocol used for Dense or Sparse Mode relies on routes discovered by an interior gateway routing protocol. In this lab, you use EIGRP. You advertise the entire 10.x.x.x network to cover all subnetworks:

```
DLRouter (config)#router eigrp 1
DLRouter (config-router)#network 10.0.0.0
```

Note: Verify using **show run**.

f. Set the PIM RP address. The RP is the root of the shared path multicast distribution tree:

```
DLRouter(config)#ip pim rp-address 10.99.1.1
```

g. Verify the complete configuration using **show run**.

Step 5

Configure the Corp router with the following information.

a. Configure the host name, Corp:

```
Router(config)#hostname Corp
```

Note: Verify using **show run**.

174

b. Enable IP multicast routing on Corp:

```
Corp(config)#ip multicast-routing
```

Note: Verify using **show run**.

c. Configure each interface with IP PIM-SM:

```
Corp(config)#interface FastEthernet0/0
Corp(config-if)#ip address 10.1.2.2 255.255.255.0
Corp(config-if)#ip pim sparse-mode

Corp(config)#interface Serial0/1
Corp(config-if)#ip address 10.99.1.1 255.255.255.0
Corp(config-if)#ip pim sparse-mode
Corp(config-if)#clockrate 128000
```

Note: Verify using **show run**.

d. Set the PIM RP address:

```
Corp(config)#ip pim rp-address 10.99.1.1
```

e. Configure the EIGRP routing protocol on the 2600. This facilitates PIM-SM multicast routing. You will also add a default route:

```
Corp(config)#router eigrp 1
Corp(config-router)#network 10.0.0.0
Corp(config-router)#redistribute static metric 64 20000 255 1 1500

Corp(config)#ip route 0.0.0.0 0.0.0.0 10.99.1.2
```

Note: Verify using **show run**.

Step 6

Configure the Branch router with the following information.

a. Configure the host name, Branch, on the external 2600 series router:

```
Router(config)#hostname Branch
```

Note: Verify using **show run**.

b. Enable IP multicast routing on Branch:

```
Branch(config)#ip multicast-routing
```

Note: Verify using **show run**.

c. Configure each interface, including necessary IP PIM processing information for the PIM-SM routing protocol. Configure CGMP on Fa0/0:

```
Branch(config)#interface FastEthernet0/0
Branch(config-if)#ip address 10.2.1.1 255.255.255.0
Branch(config-if)#ip pim sparse-mode
Branch(config-if)#ip cgmp

Branch(config)#interface Serial0/1
Branch(config-if)#ip address 10.99.1.2 255.255.255.0
Branch(config-if)#ip pim sparse-mode
```

Note: Verify using **show run**.

d. Configure the EIGRP routing protocol on the 2600. It will carry the PIM-SM multicast routing information:

```
Branch(config)#router eigrp 1Branch(config-router)#network 10.0.0.0
```

Note: Verify using **show run**.

e. Set the PIM RP address. The RP is the root of the shared path multicast distribution tree:

```
Branch(config)#ip pim rp-address 10.99.1.1
```

Note: Verify using **show run**.

Step 7

Configure ALSwitch with the following information.

a. Clear your NVRAM, and reset the switch for a clean configuration:

```
Switch#erase startSwitch#reload
```

Note: If asked to save your system configuration, enter **n** for no.

b. Configure the host name, ALSwitch, on the external 2600:

```
Switch(config)#hostname ALSwitch
```

Note: Verify using **show run**.

c. Configure CGMP leave processing on the 2900 XL:

```
ALSwitch (config)#cgmp leave-processing
```

Note: Verify using **show run**.

Step 8

Configure, connect, and test IP multicast devices and software.

a. Verify the routing tables on routers Branch and Corp. You should see entries for all networks. By looking at the Branch routing table, you also can verify that DLRouter is functioning properly. Review the examples provided next. Your table should reflect these closely:

```
Corp#show ip route

Codes: C - connected, S - static, I - IGRP, R - RIP, M - mobile, B - BGP
       D - EIGRP, EX - EIGRP external, O - OSPF, IA - OSPF inter area
       N1 - OSPF NSSA external type 1, N2 - OSPF NSSA external type 2
       E1 - OSPF external type 1, E2 - OSPF external type 2, E - EGP
       i - IS-IS, L1 - IS-IS level-1, L2 - IS-IS level-2, ia - IS-IS inter area
       * - candidate default, U - per-user static route, o - ODR
       P - periodic downloaded static route

Gateway of last resort is 10.99.1.2 to network 0.0.0.0

     10.0.0.0/24 is subnetted, 6 subnets
D        10.1.10.0 [90/28416] via 10.1.2.1, 01:09:18, FastEthernet0/0
C        10.1.3.0 is directly connected, FastEthernet0/1
D        10.2.1.0 [90/20514560] via 10.99.1.2, 00:40:30, Serial0/1
C        10.1.2.0 is directly connected, FastEthernet0/0
D        10.1.1.0 [90/28416] via 10.1.2.1, 01:09:18, FastEthernet0/0
C        10.99.1.0 is directly connected, Serial0/1
S*   0.0.0.0/0 [1/0] via 10.99.1.2
```

```
Branch#show ip route

Codes: C - connected, S - static, I - IGRP, R - RIP, M - mobile, B - BGP
       D - EIGRP, EX - EIGRP external, O - OSPF, IA - OSPF inter area
       N1 - OSPF NSSA external type 1, N2 - OSPF NSSA external type 2
       E1 - OSPF external type 1, E2 - OSPF external type 2, E - EGP
       i - IS-IS, L1 - IS-IS level-1, L2 - IS-IS level-2, ia - IS-IS inter area
       * - candidate default, U - per-user static route, o - ODR
       P - periodic downloaded static route

Gateway of last resort is 10.99.1.1 to network 0.0.0.0

     10.0.0.0/24 is subnetted, 6 subnets
D        10.1.10.0 [90/20514816] via 10.99.1.1, 00:49:28, Serial0/1
D        10.1.3.0 [90/20514560] via 10.99.1.1, 00:49:28, Serial0/1
C        10.2.1.0 is directly connected, FastEthernet0/0
D        10.1.2.0 [90/20514560] via 10.99.1.1, 00:49:28, Serial0/1
D        10.1.1.0 [90/20514816] via 10.99.1.1, 00:49:28, Serial0/1
C        10.99.1.0 is directly connected, Serial0/1
D*EX 0.0.0.0/0 [170/45632000] via 10.99.1.1, 00:49:28, Serial0/1
```

b. Connect the IP/TV multicast server to any VLAN 10 port on the 4006 switch (ports 2/19–24). Ensure that the IP address of the multicast server is set to 10.1.10.2/24 with a gateway of 10.1.10.1.

Use the **ipconfig** or **winipcfg** command from the DOS prompt to verify your entries.

c. From a command prompt on the multicast server, use the **ping** command to test your ability to reach the gateway IP address 10.1.10.1 and the Branch network gateway address:

```
C:\>ping 10.1.10.1

C:\>ping 10.2.1.1
```

Note: If these **ping** commands do not function, you need to troubleshoot the problem before continuing.

d. On the IP/TV multicast server, activate the IP/TV media server software. Right-click the multicast stream **Corporate Communications** and select **Enable/Disable Program**, as shown in the following figure. Ensure that the green activation indicator is displayed on the software management screen.

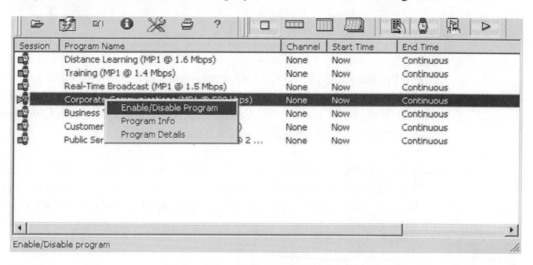

e. Connect the IP/TV multicast client PC to interface Fa0/2 on ALSwitch. Ensure that the IP address of the client PC is set to 10.2.1.2/24 with a gateway of 10.2.1.1.

Use the **ipconfig** or **winipcfg** command from the DOS prompt to verify your entries.

f. From a command prompt on the multicast client, use the **ping** command to test your ability to reach the multicast server IP address 10.1.10.2:

```
C:\>ping 10.1.10.2
```

Note: If these **ping** commands do not function, you need to troubleshoot the problem before continuing.

g. On the IP/TV multicast client, activate the IP/TV viewer software. Ensure that the Content Manager settings are configured as shown in the following figure.

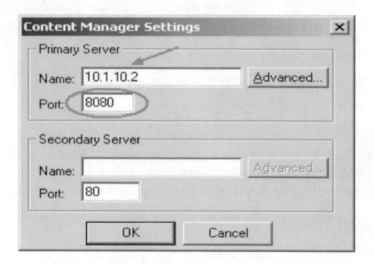

h. Refresh the screen on the IP/TV viewer. Remember that you want to receive *audio only*. So instead of double-clicking, right-click and select **Stream**. Uncheck **Video** and leave only **Audio** selected. Click **OK**. John Chambers' speech should start playing the stream produced by the server.

Note: If the stream does not start playing, you should stop and restart the stream from the IP/TV server. If it still does not start, there is a problem. Use the next section to help in your troubleshooting, because multicast routing is difficult to troubleshoot.

Step 9

Investigate and troubleshoot multicast routing. You should activate the stream on the client before executing these commands. This allows the extraction of useful troubleshooting information.

a. Show the multicast routing table on DLRouter, Corp, and Branch. Viewing the multicast routing table is the primary means of troubleshooting IP multicast routing. It displays several items, including routing, PIM, and stream information:

```
DLRouter#show ip mroute
```

1. What is the RP for DLRouter?

2. What does it mean if nothing is displayed?

_____

```
Corp#show ip mroute

Branch#show ip mroute
```

b. Show PIM neighbor information. This command lets you verify the PIM mode used, along with the modes used by neighbors.

```
DLRouter#show ip pim neighbor
```

3. What PIM neighbor is displayed?

_____

```
DLRouter#show ip pim interface
```

Complete the following table:

Address	Interface	Version/Mode	Nbr	Query Count	DR Intvl
_____	Port-channel1	v2/Sparse	0	30	
_____	Port-channel1.2	v2/Sparse	1	30	_____
_____	Port-channel1.10	v2/Sparse	0	30	_____
_____	Port-channel1.20	v2/Sparse	0	30	_____
_____	Port-channel1.30	v2/Sparse	0	30	_____

```
Corp#show ip pim neighbor
```

4. Which PIM neighbors are displayed?

_____

```
Branch#show ip pim neighbor
```

5. Which PIM neighbor is displayed?

_____

```
Branch#show ip pim interface
```

Complete the following table:

Address	Interface	Version/Mode	Nbr	Query Count	DR Intvl
_____	FastEthernet0/0	v2/Sparse	0	30	_____
_____	Serial0/1	v2/Sparse	1	30	_____

c. Show PIM RP information. This command lets you verify the PIM group-to-RP mappings for the data streams.

```
Branch#show ip pim rp mapping
```

6. What are the group multicast addresses?

---

d. Check some miscellaneous information. These commands are often used in addition to the preceding commands for multicast troubleshooting. You do not ask any additional questions in these commands; however, you should compare your results and identify items that might assist you in multicast troubleshooting:

```
DLRouter#show ip pim interface count

State: * - Fast Switched, D - Distributed Fast Switched
       H - Hardware Switched
Address          Interface          FS  Mpackets In/Out
10.1.1.1         Port-channel1      *   0/0
10.1.2.1         Port-channel1.2    *   989/909
10.1.10.1        Port-channel1.10   *   909/8
10.1.20.1        Port-channel1.20   *   0/0
10.1.30.1        Port-channel1.30   *   0/0
```

```
Corp#show ip pim interface

Address      Interface       Version/Mode  Nbr  Query  DR
                                                Count  Intvl
10.1.2.2     FastEthernet0/0 v2/Dense      1    30     10.1.2.2
10.1.3.1     FastEthernet0/1 v2/Dense      0    30     10.1.3.1
10.99.1.1    Serial0/1       v2/Sparse     1    30     0.0.0.0
```

```
Corp#sh ip pim interface count

State: * - Fast Switched, D - Distributed Fast Switched
       H - Hardware Switched
Address          Interface          FS  Mpackets In/Out
10.1.2.2         FastEthernet0/0    *   206330/1202
10.1.3.1         FastEthernet0/1    *   441/90576
10.99.1.1        Serial0/1          *   1418/108439
```

```
Corp#show ip igmp groups

IGMP Connected Group Membership
Group Address    Interface          Uptime    Expires  Last Reporter
224.0.1.40       FastEthernet0/1    01:11:19  never    10.1.3.1
```

```
Corp#debug ip pim auto-rp
PIM Auto-RP debugging is on
```

```
Branch#show ip pim interface count

State: * - Fast Switched, D - Distributed Fast Switched
       H - Hardware Switched

Address          Interface          FS  Mpackets In/Out
10.2.1.1         FastEthernet0/0    *   710/25787
10.99.1.2        Serial0/1          *   26575/706
```

```
Branch#show ip igmp groups

IGMP Connected Group Membership
Group Address    Interface          Uptime    Expires   Last Reporter
224.0.1.40       Serial0/1          00:40:25  never     0.0.0.0
239.255.151.121  FastEthernet0/0    00:32:25  00:02:54  10.2.1.2
```

7. What commands have you determined would be the most helpful in troubleshooting multicast routing?

_____

_____
_____

_____

    This lab demonstrated how to configure PIM-SM for use with a multicast server and multicast clients in a campus LAN.

Lab 10-1: Local Switch Security for Controlled User Access

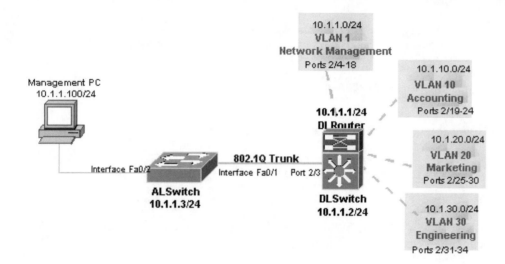

Objective

Use local switch security for controlled user access.

Scenario

Your network consists of several network devices. You want to configure access security to your devices. You do *not* have a TACACS+ or RADIUS server available for centralized access. Configure each device as required. Use the following security information:

Local Passwords
User: admin
Password: cisco
Enable secret: class

Step 1

Cable the lab as shown in the diagram.

Step 2

The first device to be configured is the Catalyst 2900 XL. Log into the switch, enter privileged mode, clear the NVRAM, and restart.

Step 3

Configure ALSwitch, including basic information and trunking information.

a. Configure the host name:

```
Switch(config)#hostname ALSwitch
```

b. Configure the switch trunking information on FastEthernet0/1 and PortFast on FastEthernet0/2:

```
ALSwitch(config)#interface FastEthernet0/1
ALSwitch(config-if)#switchport trunk encapsulation dot1q
ALSwitch(config-if)#switchport mode trunk

ALSwitch(config)#interface FastEthernet0/2
ALSwitch(config-if)#spanning-tree portfast
```

c. Configure the in-band management interface with an IP address:

```
ALSwitch(config)#interface VLAN1
ALSwitch(config-if)#ip address 10.1.1.3 255.255.255.0
```

Step 4

Configure ALSwitch for Authentication, Authorization, and Accounting (AAA) with local authentication as a backup to TACACS+.

a. Configure local authentication:

```
ALSwitch(config)#aaa new-model
ALSwitch(config)#aaa authentication login default group tacacs+ local
ALSwitch(config)#aaa authentication enable default group tacacs+ enable
```

b. Configure a local admin user account:

```
ALSwitch(config)#username admin password cisco
```

c. Configure a local enable secret password:

```
ALSwitch(config)#enable secret enable
```

Step 5

The next device to be configured is the Catalyst 4006 L3 module. From the console port on the L3 module, log into the router, enter privileged mode, clear the NVRAM, and then restart.

Step 6

Configure the DLRouter, including all basic information and trunking information.

a. Configure the host name:

```
Router(config)#hostname DLRouter
```

b. Configure the basic connectivity information, including IP addressing and trunking:

```
DLRouter(config)#interface Port-channel1
DLRouter(config-if)#ip address 10.1.1.1 255.255.255.0
```

```
DLRouter(config)#interface Port-channel1.10
DLRouter(config-if)#encapsulation dot1Q 10
DLRouter(config-if)#ip address 10.1.10.1 255.255.255.0

DLRouter(config)#interface Port-channel1.20
DLRouter(config-if)#encapsulation dot1Q 20
DLRouter(config-if)#ip address 10.1.20.1 255.255.255.0

DLRouter(config)#interface Port-channel1.30
DLRouter(config-if)#encapsulation dot1Q 30
DLRouter(config-if)#ip address 10.1.30.1 255.255.255.0

DLRouter(config)#interface GigabitEthernet3
DLRouter(config-if)#no ip address
DLRouter(config-if)#channel-group 1

DLRouter(config)#interface GigabitEthernet4
DLRouter(config-if)#no ip address
DLRouter(config-if)#channel-group 1
```

Step 7

Configure the DLRouter for AAA, with local authentication as a backup to
TACACS+.

a. Configure local authentication:

```
DLRouter(config)#aaa new-model
DLRouter(config)#aaa authentication login default group tacacs+ local
```

b. Configure a local admin user account:

```
DLRouter(config)#username admin password cisco
```

c. Configure a local enable secret password:

```
DLRouter(config)#enable secret class
```

Step 8

The next device to be configured is DLSwitch. From the console port on the
switch, log into the switch, enter privileged mode, clear the NVRAM, and restart.

Step 9

Configure DLSwitch, including all basic information and trunking information.

a. Configure the host name:

```
Console> (enable) set system name DLSwitch
```

b. Configure other basic information:

```
DLSwitch> (enable) set vtp domain Corp
DLSwitch> (enable) set vtp mode server
DLSwitch> (enable) set vlan 1 name default
DLSwitch> (enable) set vlan 10 name Accounting
DLSwitch> (enable) set vlan 20 name Marketing
```

```
DLSwitch> (enable) set vlan 30 name Engineering
DLSwitch> (enable) set interface sc0 1 10.1.1.2/255.255.255.0 10.1.1.255
DLSwitch> (enable) set ip route 0.0.0.0/0.0.0.0 10.1.1.1
DLSwitch> (enable) set port channel 2/1-2 156
DLSwitch> (enable) set vlan 10 2/19-24
DLSwitch> (enable) set vlan 20 2/25-30
DLSwitch> (enable) set vlan 30 2/31-34
DLSwitch> (enable) set trunk 2/1 nonegotiate dot1q 1-1005
DLSwitch> (enable) set trunk 2/2 nonegotiate dot1q 1-1005
DLSwitch> (enable) set trunk 2/3 nonegotiate dot1q 1-1005
DLSwitch> (enable) set port channel 2/1-2 mode on
```

c. Configure local security. Notice that you set only local access passwords, not users:

```
DLSwitch> (enable) set password {set this to 'cisco'}
DLSwitch> (enable) set enablepass {set this to 'enable'}
```

Step 10

Test authentication.

Connect to the console port of each switch. Use the user ID and passwords assigned for each switch to test authentication. Enable the following on each AAA-enabled device, and answer the following questions:

```
debug tacacs
debug aaa authentication
```

1. On ALSwitch or DLRouter, what is the AAA authentication START method?

_____

_____

_____

2. On ALSwitch or DLRouter, what is the AAA/TACACS START method?

_____

_____

_____

3. When you're debugging AAA authentication, does the password display as part of the debug information?

_____

4. On ALSwitch or DLRouter, which AAA/CONT method is used to access privileged mode?

_____

_____

_____

This lab demonstrated how to configure local authentication as a backup authentication method for TACACS+.

Lab 10-2: CiscoSecure ACS Switch Security for Controlled User Access

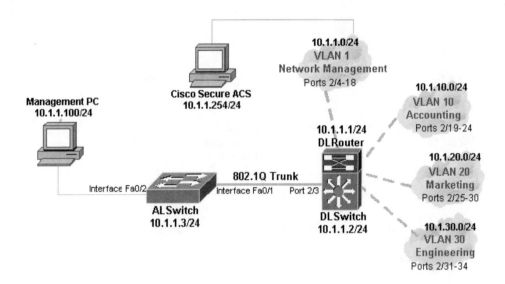

Objective

Use CiscoSecure Access Control Server (ACS) security for controlled user access.

Scenario

Your network consists of several network devices. You want to configure access security to your devices. You have CiscoSecure Server for centralized authentication using the TACACS+ protocol. Configure each device for secure access while also configuring local access as a fallback in case the ACS server is unavailable. Use the following information:

TACACS+ (These Must Be Created on the ACS Server Prior to This Lab)
User: smith
Password: cisco
Enable password: tacacs
Key: superman

Local
User: admin
Password: cisco
Enable password: class

Step 1

Cable the lab as shown in the diagram.

Step 2

The first device to be configured is the Catalyst 2900 XL. Log into the switch, enter privileged mode, clear the NVRAM, and restart.

Step 3

Configure ALSwitch, including basic information and trunking information.

a. Configure the host name:

```
Switch(config)#hostname ALSwitch
```

b. Configure the switch trunking information on FastEthernet0/1 and PortFast on FastEthernet0/2:

```
ALSwitch(config)#interface FastEthernet0/1
ALSwitch(config-if)#switchport trunk encapsulation dot1q
ALSwitch(config-if)#switchport mode trunk

ALSwitch(config)#interface FastEthernet0/2
ALSwitch(config-if)#spanning-tree portfast
```

c. Configure the in-band management interface with an IP address:

```
ALSwitch(config)#interface VLAN1
ALSwitch(config-if)#ip address 10.1.1.3 255.255.255.0
```

Step 4

Configure ALSwitch for AAA with local authentication as a backup for TACACS+.

a. Configure authentication for the login, and enable access:

```
ALSwitch(config)#aaa new-model
ALSwitch(config)#aaa authentication login default group tacacs+ local
ALSwitch(config)#aaa authentication enable default group tacacs+ enable
```

b. Configure TACACS+ commands for ACS authentication:

```
ALSwitch(config)#tacacs-server host 10.1.1.254
ALSwitch(config)#tacacs-server timeout 30
ALSwitch(config)#tacacs-server key superman
```

c. Configure a local admin user account:

```
ALSwitch(config)#username admin password cisco
```

d. Configure a local enable secret password:

```
ALSwitch(config)#enable secret class
```

Step 5

The next device to be configured is the Catalyst 4006 L3 Module. From the console port on the L3 module, log into the router, enter privileged mode, clear the NVRAM, and restart.

Step 6

Configure the DLRouter, including all basic information and trunking information.

a. Configure the host name:

```
Router(config)#hostname DLRouter
```

b. Configure the basic connectivity information, including IP addressing and trunking:

```
DLRouter(config)#interface Port-channel1
DLRouter(config-if)#ip address 10.1.1.1 255.255.255.0

DLRouter(config)#interface Port-channel1.10
DLRouter(config-if)#encapsulation dot1Q 10
DLRouter(config-if)#ip address 10.1.10.1 255.255.255.0

DLRouter(config)#interface Port-channel1.20
DLRouter(config-if)#encapsulation dot1Q 20
DLRouter(config-if)#ip address 10.1.20.1 255.255.255.0

DLRouter(config)#interface Port-channel1.30
DLRouter(config-if)#encapsulation dot1Q 30
DLRouter(config-if)#ip address 10.1.30.1 255.255.255.0

DLRouter(config)#interface GigabitEthernet3
DLRouter(config-if)#no ip address
DLRouter(config-if)#channel-group 1

DLRouter(config)#interface GigabitEthernet4
DLRouter(config-if)#no ip address
DLRouter(config-if)#channel-group 1
```

Step 7

Configure AAA on the DLRouter.

a. Configure the security for local login and enable access:

```
DLRouter(config)#aaa new-model
DLRouter(config)#aaa authentication login default tacacs+ local
DLRouter(config)#aaa authentication enable default tacacs+ enable
```

b. Configure the security for ACS authentication:

```
DLRouter(config)#tacacs-server host 10.1.1.254
DLRouter(config)#tacacs-server timeout 30
DLRouter(config)#tacacs-server key superman
```

c. Configure a local admin user account:

```
DLRouter(config)#username admin password cisco
```

d. Configure a local enable secret password:

```
DLRouter(config)#enable secret enable
```

Step 8

The next device to be configured is DLSwitch. From the console port on the switch, log into the switch, enter privileged mode, clear the NVRAM, and restart.

Step 9

Configure DLSwitch, including all basic information and trunking information.

a. Configure the host name:

```
Console>(enable) set system name DLSwitch>
```

b. Configure other basic information:

```
DLSwitch>(enable) set vtp domain Corp
DLSwitch>(enable) set vtp mode server
DLSwitch>(enable) set vlan 1 name default
DLSwitch>(enable) set vlan 10 name Accounting
DLSwitch>(enable) set vlan 20 name Marketing
DLSwitch>(enable) set vlan 30 name Engineering
DLSwitch>(enable) set interface sc0 1 10.1.1.2/255.255.255.0 10.1.1.255
DLSwitch>(enable) set ip route 0.0.0.0/0.0.0.0 10.1.1.1
DLSwitch>(enable) set port channel 2/1-2 156
DLSwitch>(enable) set vlan 10 2/19-24
DLSwitch>(enable) set vlan 20 2/25-30
DLSwitch>(enable) set vlan 30 2/31-34
DLSwitch>(enable) set trunk 2/1 nonegotiate dot1q 1-1005
DLSwitch>(enable) set trunk 2/2 nonegotiate dot1q 1-1005
DLSwitch>(enable) set trunk 2/3 nonegotiate dot1q 1-1005
DLSwitch>(enable) set port channel 2/1-2 mode on
DLSwitch>(enable) set spantree portfast 2/4 enable
```

c. Configure local security. Notice that you set only local access passwords, not users:

```
DLSwitch>(enable) set password {set this to 'cisco'}
DLSwitch>(enable) set enablepass {set this to 'enable'}
```

d. Configure ACS security:

```
DLSwitch>(enable) set tacacs server 10.1.1.254 primary
DLSwitch>(enable) set tacacs key superman
DLSwitch>(enable) set tacacs timeout 30
DLSwitch>(enable) set authentication login tacacs enable
DLSwitch>(enable) set authentication enable tacacs enable
```

Step 10

Test authentication.

Connect to the console port of each switch. Use the user ID and passwords assigned for each switch to test authentication. Enable the following on each of the AAA enabled devices, and answer the following questions.
For DLRouter and ALSwitch, use the following:

```
debug tacacs
debug aaa authentication
```

For DLSwitch, use the following:

```
set trace tacacs
```

1. What command disables tracing on the 4006 switch?

_____

2. On each switch or router, can you log on using local authentication if TACACS authentication is functioning?

_____

3. Disconnect the ACS server from the network. Can you log on locally? Reconnect after this step is complete.

_____

This lab demonstrated how to configure Catalyst switches with AAA and TACACS+ for centralized authentication from a CiscoSecure ACS.

Appendix A

Command Reference

Chapter 3: Switch Administration

Viewing and Clearing a Configuration

IOS-Based Switch

```
Switch#show running-config

Switch#erase startup-config

Switch#delete vlan.dat
```

CatOS Switch

```
Switch> (enable) show config

Switch> (enable) clear config all
```

Setting a Password

IOS-Based Switch

Set EXEC-Level Password
```
Switch(config)#enable password level 1 password
```

Set Privileged-Level Password
```
Switch(config)#enable password level 15 password

Switch(config)#enable secret password
```

CatOS Switch

Set Privileged-Level Password
```
Switch> (enable) set enablepass
```

Set Normal-Mode, vty, and Console Passwords
```
Switch> (enable) set password
```

Naming the Switch

IOS-Based Switch

```
Switch(config)#hostname hostname
```

CatOS Switch

```
Switch> (enable) set system name name-string

Switch> (enable) set prompt name
```

Configuring the Switch for Remote Access

IOS-Based Switch

In-Band Management VLAN

```
Switch(config)#interface vlan x

Switch(config-if)#ip address ip-address netmask

Switch(config-if)#ip default-gateway ip-address

Switch#show ip interface
```

CatOS Switch

In-Band Management VLAN

```
Switch> (enable) set interface sc0 up

Switch> (enable) set interface sc0 ip-address netmask broadcast

Switch> (enable) set interface sc0 vlan

Switch> (enable) set ip route default gateway-address

Switch> (enable) show interface
```

Identifying Individual Ports

IOS-Based Switch

```
Switch(config-if)#description description-string
```

CatOS Switch

```
Switch> (enable) set port name mod/num description

Switch> (enable) show port name mod/num
```

Defining Link Speed

IOS-Based Switch

```
Switch(config-if)#speed [10 | 100 | auto]
```

CatOS Switch

```
Switch> (enable) set port speed mod/num [10 | 100 | auto]
```

Defining Line Mode on a Switch

IOS-Based Switch

```
Switch(config-if)#duplex [auto | full | half]
```

CatOS Switch

```
Switch> (enable) set port duplex mod/num [auto | full | half]

Switch> (enable) set port enable mod/num
```

Setting Idle Timeout

IOS-Based Switch

```
Switch(config-line)#exec-timeout minutes
```

CatOS Switch

```
Switch> (enable) set logout minutes
```

Verifying Connectivity

IOS-Based Switch

```
Switch#ping ip-address
```

CatOS Switch

```
Switch> (enable) ping ip-address
```

Backing Up and Restoring a Configuration Using a TFTP Server

CatOS Switch

```
Switch> (enable) write net (upload)

Switch> (enable) configure net (download)

Switch> (enable) copy config [flash | file-id | tftp]

Switch> (enable) copy flash [flash | file-id | config]
```

HTTP Switch Commands

CatOS Switch

```
Switch> (enable) set ip http server enable

Switch> (enable) set ip http port port-number default

Switch> (enable) set authentication login

Switch> (enable) show authentication
```

Chapter 4: Introduction to VLANs

Configuring Static VLANs

IOS-Based Switch

```
Switch(config-if)#switchport mode [access | multi | trunk]

Switch(config-if)#switchport access vlan vlan-num
```

CatOS Switch

```
Switch> (enable) set vlan vlan-num mod/num,list
```

Verifying VLAN Configuration

IOS-Based Switch

```
Switch#show vlan brief
```

CatOS Switch

```
Switch> (enable) show vlan
```

Deleting VLANs

IOS-Based Switch

```
Switch(vlan)#no vlan vlan-id
```

CatOS Switch

```
Switch> (enable) clear vlan vlan
```

Configuring the VMPS Server

CatOS Switch

```
Switch> (config) set vmps state enable

Switch> (config) set vmps state disable
```

Configuring a VMPS Client

CatOS Switch

```
Switch> (enable) set vmps server ip-address [primary]

Switch> (enable) show vmps server

Switch> (enable) set port membership mod-num port-num {dynamic | static}
Switch> (enable) show port {mod-num/port-num}
```

Configuring a VLAN Trunk

IOS-Based Switch

```
Switch(config-if)#switchport mode [access | multi | trunk]

Switch(config-if)#switchport trunk encapsulation {isl | dot1q}
```

CatOS Switch

```
Switch> (enable) set trunk mod/port [on | off | desirable | auto | nonegotiate]
  [isl | dot1q | dot10 | lane | negotiate] vlan-range

Switch> (enable) show port capabilities mod/num
```

Removing VLANs from a Trunk

IOS-Based Switch

```
Switch(config-if)#switchport trunk allowed vlan remove vlan-list
```

CatOS Switch

```
Switch> (enable) clear trunk mod/port vlan-range
```

```
Switch> (enable) show trunk
```

Configuring the VTP Version

IOS-Based Switch

```
Switch(vlan)#vtp v2-mode
```

CatOS Switch

```
Switch> (enable) set vtp v2 enable (version 2)
```

Configuring the VTP Domain

IOS-Based Switch

```
Switch(vlan)#vtp domain domain-name
```

CatOS Switch

```
Switch> (enable) set vtp [domain domain-name] [mode {server | client |
  transparent}] [password password]
```

Configuring the VTP Mode

IOS-Based Switch

```
Switch(vlan)#vtp {server | client | transparent}
```

CatOS Switch

```
Switch> (enable) set vtp [domain domain-name] [mode {server | client |
  transparent}] [password password]
```

Verifying VTP Configuration

IOS-Based Switch

```
Switch#show vtp
```

```
Switch#show vtp status
```

```
Switch#show vtp counters
```

CatOS Switch

```
Switch> (enable) show vtp domain
```

```
Switch> (enable) show vtp statistics
```

```
Switch> (enable) show vlan
```

Configuring VTP Pruning

IOS-Based Switch

```
Switch(vlan)#vtp pruning

Switch(config-if)#switchport trunk pruning vlan remove vlan-list
```

CatOS Switch

```
Switch> (enable) set vtp pruning enable

Switch> (enable) set vtp pruneeligible vlan-range

Switch> (enable) clear vtp pruning vlan-range
```

Verifying VTP Pruning

IOS-Based Switch

```
Switch#show interface mod/num switchport

Switch#show vtp

Switch#show vtp status

Switch#show vtp counters
```

CatOS Switch

```
Switch> (enable) show trunk

Switch> (enable) show vtp domain

Switch> (enable) show vtp statistics
```

Chapter 5: Spanning Tree Protocol

Enabling and Verifying Spanning Tree

IOS-Based Switch

```
Switch(config)#spantree vlan-list

Switch(config)#no spantree vlan-list

Switch#show spanning-tree [vlan]

Switch#show spanning-tree mod/num
```

CatOS Switch

```
Switch> (enable) set spantree enable [all | mod/num]

Switch> (enable) set spantree disable [all | mod/num]

Switch> (enable) show spantree [vlan]

Switch> (enable) show spantree mod/num
```

Establishing a Root Bridge

IOS-Based Switch

```
Switch(config)#spanning-tree portfast
```

```
Switch(config)#spanning-tree [vlan vlan-list] priority priority
```

CatOS Switch

```
Switch> (enable) set spantree root [secondary] [vlan-list] [dia diameter]
  [hello hellotime]
```

Configuring the Root Cost

IOS-Based Switch

```
Switch(config-if)#spanning-tree [vlan vlan-list] cost cost
```

CatOS Switch

```
Switch> (enable) set spantree portcost mod/num cost
```

```
Switch> (enable) set spantree portvlancost mod/num [cost cost] [vlan-list]
```

Modifying Port Priority

IOS-Based Switch

```
Switch(config-if)#spanning-tree [vlan vlan-list] port-priority port-priority
```

CatOS Switch

```
Switch> (enable) set spantree portpri mod/num cost
```

Modifying Port Priority by VLAN

IOS-Based Switch

```
Switch(config-if)#spanning-tree [vlan vlan-list] port-priority port-priority
```

CatOS Switch

```
Switch> (enable) set spantree portvlanpri mod/num priority vlan-list
```

Modifying STP Timers

IOS-Based Switch

```
Switch(config)#spanning-tree [vlan vlan-list] [hello-time seconds]
```

```
Switch(config)#spanning-tree [vlan vlan-list] [forward-time seconds]
```

```
Switch(config)#spanning-tree [vlan vlan-list] [max-age seconds]
```

CatOS Switch

```
Switch> (enable) set spantree hello interval [vlan]

Switch> (enable) set spantree fwddelay delay [vlan]

Switch> (enable) set spantree maxage agingtime [vlan]

Switch> (enable) set spantree root [secondary] [vlan-list] [dia diameter]
   [hello hellotime]
```

Configuring Fast EtherChannel

IOS-Based Switch

```
Switch(config-if)#port group group number distribution destination | source
```

CatOS Switch

```
Switch> (enable) show port capabilities [mod_num[/port_num]]

Switch> (enable) set port channel mod_num/ports on | off | auto | desirable
```

Configuring PortFast

IOS-Based Switch

```
Switch(config)#spanning-tree portfast
```

CatOS Switch

```
Switch> (enable) set spantree portfast [mod/num] [enable | disable]
```

Configuring UplinkFast

IOS-Based Switch

```
Switch(config)#spanning-tree uplinkfast [max-update-rate pkts-per-sec]
```

CatOS Switch

```
Switch> (enable) set spantree uplinkfast [enable | disable] [rate update-rate]
   [all-protocols off | on]
```

Configuring BackboneFast

IOS-Based Switch

```
Switch(config)#spanning-tree backbonefast
```

CatOS Switch

```
Switch> (enable) set spantree backbonefast [enable | disable]

Switch> (enable) show spantree backbonefast
```

Chapter 6: Inter-VLAN Routing

Accessing the Route Processor

CatOS Switch

```
Switch(enable) show module

Switch(enable) session module-number

Router(config)# hostname name
```

Configuring a Routing Protocol on the Route Processor

```
Router(config)#ip routing

Router(config)#router routing-protocol

Router(config-router)#network network
```

Configuring Route Processor Interfaces

```
Router(config)# interface vlan-interface-number

Router(config-if)# ip address ip-address subnet-mask

Router(config)# interface port-channel channel_number

Router(config)# interface [g3 | g4]

Router(config-if)# channel-group channel_number

Router(config)# interface port-channel channel_number.vlan_id

Router(config-subif)# encapsulation dot1Q vlan_id

Router(config-subif)# ip address ip_address subnet_mask

Router(config)# interface port-channel channel_number.vlan_id

Router(config-subif)# encapsulation dot1Q vlan_id native

Router(config-subif)# ip address ip_address subnet_mask

Switch (enable) set port channel mod_num/ports on | off | auto | desirable

Switch (enable) set trunk mod_num/port_num
```

Configuring a Default Gateway on a Switch

IOS-Based Switch

```
Switch(config)#ip default-gateway ip-address
```

CatOS Switch

```
Switch> (enable) set ip route destination gateway metric
```

Configuring External Routers

```
Router(config)#interface ethernet slot-number/port-number.subinterface-number

Router(config-if)#encapsulation isl vlan-number

Router(config-if)#ip address ip-address subnet-mask
```

Chapter 7: Multilayer Switching

Verifying that MLS Packets Are Sent by the MLS-RP

CatOS Switch

```
Switch> (enable) show cam
```

Cache Aging Issues

CatOS Switch

```
Console> (enable) set mls agingtime [agingtime]

Console> (enable) set mls agingtime fast [fastagingtime] [pkt_threshold]
```

Configuring the Route Processor

```
Router(config)#mls rp ip

Router(config)#interface vlan vlan-number

Router(config-if)#mls rp vtp-domain domain-name

Router(config-if)#mls rp management-interface
```

Configuring MLS for a VTP Domain

```
Router(config)#interface ethernet 0

Router(config-if)#mls rp vlan-id vlan-id-num

Router(config-if)#mls rp vtp-domain domain-name

Router(config-if)#mls rp ip
```

Enabling MLS on an Interface

```
Router(config-if)#mls rp ip
```

MLS Management Interface

```
Router(config-if)#mls rp management-interface
```

Assigning a VLAN ID to an Interface on an External Router

```
Router(config)#interface interface

Router(config-if)#mls rp vlan-id vlan-id-num
```

Input Access Lists and Flow Masks

```
Router(config)#mls rp input-acl
```

Enabling and Disabling MLS on a Switch
CatOS Switch

```
Switch> (enable) set mls enable

Switch> (enable) set mls disable
```

Adding External Router MLS Identification
CatOS Switch

```
Switch> (enable) set mls include ip-address

Switch> (enable) show mls rp

Switch> (enable) clear mls include
```

Verifying MLS Configuration
CatOS Switch

```
Switch> (enable) show mls

Switch> (enable) show mls include

Switch> (enable) show mls entry source

Switch> (enable) show mls entry destination

Switch> (enable) show mls entry flow

Switch> (enable) show mls entry rp

Switch> (enable) clear mls entry source ip-address

Switch> (enable) clear mls entry destination ip-address

Switch> (enable) clear mls entry rp ip-address

Switch> (enable) clear mls entry flow protocol source-port destination-port
```

Chapter 8: Hot Standby Router Protocol

Viewing the Virtual Router MAC Address

```
Router#show ip arp
```

Configuring HSRP

```
Router(config-if)#standby group-num ip virtual-ip-add
```

HSRP Standby Priority

```
Router(config-if)#standby group-num priority priority
```

HSRP Standby Preempt

```
Router(config-if)#standby group-num preempt
```

HSRP Hello Timers

```
Router(config-if)#standby group-num timers hellotime holdtime
```

HSRP Interface Tracking

```
Router(config-if)#standby group-num track type num decremented-priority
```

Verifying HSRP Configuration

```
Router#show standby type group brief
```

```
Router#show standby brief
```

Chapter 9: Multicasting

Configuring PIM-DM

```
Router(config)#ip multicast-routing
```

```
Router(config)#ip pim {dense-mode | sparse-mode | sparse-dense-mode}
```

Configuring PIM-SM

```
Router(config)#ip multicast-routing
```

```
Router(config)#ip pim {dense-mode | sparse-mode | sparse-dense-mode}
```

```
Router(config)#ip pim rp-address ip-address [group-acl-num] [override]
```

Verifying PIM Configuration

```
Router#show ip pim interface [type number] [count]
```

Displaying a PIM Neighbor

```
Router#show ip pim neighbor [type] [number]
```

Configuring Auto-RP

```
Router(config)#ip pim send-rp-announce type number scope ttl group-list
  acl-number
```

```
Router(config)#ip pim send-rp-discover scope ttl
```

Defining the Scope of Delivery of Multicast Packets

```
Router(config-if)#ip multicast ttl-threshold ttl
```

Joining a Multicast Group

```
Router(config-if)#ip igmp join-group group-address
```

Changing IGMP Versions

```
Router#show ip igmp interface type-number
```

```
Router(config-if)#ip igmp version {2 | 1}
```

Configuring CGMP

```
Router(config-if)#ip cgmp
```

IOS-Based Switch

```
Switch(config)#cgmp (CGMP enabled by default)
```

```
Switch(config)#cgmp leave-processing
```

CatOS Switch

```
Switch> (enable) set cgmp enable
```

Configuring CGMP Leave

CatOS Switch

```
Switch> (enable) show cgmp leave
```

```
Switch> (enable) set cgmp leave enable
```

```
Switch> (enable) set cgmp leave disable
```

Verifying CGMP Configuration

IOS-Based Switch

```
Switch#show cgmp
```

CatOS Switch

```
Switch> (enable) show cgmp statistics vlan
```

```
Switch> (enable) show multicast group cgmp vlan
```

Chapter 10: Security

Basic Password Protection

IOS-Based Switch

Set EXEC-Level Password
```
Switch(config)#enable password level 1 password
```

Set Privileged-Level Password
```
Switch(config)#enable password level 15 password
```

```
Switch(config)#username username password password
```

```
Switch(config-line)#login local
```

```
Switch(config-line)#login authentication
```

```
Switch(config-line)#login tacacs
```

CatOS Switch

```
Switch> (enable) set enablepass
```

```
Switch> (enable) set password
```

Using AAA and Secure Server

CatOS Switch

```
Switch> (enable) set authentication login local enable
```

```
Switch> (enable) set authentication login tacacs enable
```

```
Switch> (enable) set tacacs server ip-address
```

```
Switch> (enable) set tacacs key key
```

Restricting VTY and HTTP Access

IOS-Based Switch

```
Switch(config)#ip http server
```

```
Switch(config)#ip http authentication [aaa | enable | local | tacacs]
```

```
Switch(config-line)#access-class number in | out
```

CatOS Switch

```
Switch> (enable) set interface sc0 [ip_addr/netmask]
```

```
Switch> (enable) set ip http server enable
```

```
Switch> (enable) set ip http port port_number default
```

```
Switch> (enable) show ip http
```

Configuring Timeouts

IOS-Based Switch

```
Switch(config-line)#exec-timeout minutes
```

CatOS Switch

```
Switch> (enable) set logout [number of minutes]
```

Configuring Privilege Levels

```
Router(config)#privilege mode level level command

Router(config)#enable secret level level password
```

Banner Messages

```
Router(config)#banner motd % message here %
```

CatOS Switch

```
Switch> (enable) set banner motd % message here %
```

Policy in the Access Layer

IOS-Based Switch

```
Switch(config-if)#port security [max-mac-count maximum-mac-count]

Switch#show mac-address-table security [type module/port]

Switch(config-if)#port security action shutdown
```

CatOS Switch

```
Switch> (enable) set port security mod_num/port_num... enable mac address

Switch> (enable) show port mod_num/port_num
```

Appendix B

Cisco IOS, CatOS, and CatIOS

Cisco Systems is migrating chassis-based Catalyst switches to the CatIOS, which permits a single image to be used on a Supervisor Engine. This is the case for a Catalyst 6000 family switch with an MSFC or MSFC2. This is also the case for the image used on the Catalyst 4006 and 4500 switch with the Supervisor Engine III or Supervisor Engine IV, which has an integrated route processor. In addition, CatIOS commands are used on 7600 series Internet routers, which serve as an evolutionary upgrade to Cisco 7200 and 7500 series routers, with comprehensive support for optical MAN and WAN functionality.

CatIOS is sometimes used to refer to the operating systems used on IOS-based Catalyst switches, such as the 2900 XL, 3500 XL, 2950, and 3550 switches.

CatIOS can also be used to refer to the operating system used with the 16- and 36-port Ethernet Switch Module on Cisco 2600 series, Cisco 3600 series, and Cisco 3700 series routers: Cisco IOS Release 12.2(2)XT and later.

The CatIOS terminology is convenient because basically, it refers to the use of Cisco IOS commands but implies the addition of a series of other commands that are specific to the switching functionality of the Catalyst device or Cisco router (such as a Cisco 7600 series router). The specific additional commands are necessarily somewhat dependent on the individual platform.

A convergence is definitely taking place with the lists of commands used by various Cisco devices. This is the whole idea. It makes the use of Cisco devices much easier in general and does not require the customer to learn multiple operating systems and command sets.

One side effect of this evolution is the demise of CatOS. Although CatOS devices will remain in the field for some time, eventually the use of CatOS on these devices will end or the devices will be replaced by CatIOS devices. In particular, the Catalyst 4006 switch with Supervisor Engine II, the Catalyst 5000 Family of switches, and the Catalyst 6000 Family of switches running CatOS are being replaced by the Catalyst 4006 and 4500 switches with Supervisor Engine III or IV and the Catalyst 6000 Family of switches running CatIOS.

Because the Catalyst 1900 Enterprise Edition, 2820 Enterprise Edition, 2900 XL, 2950, 3500 XL, and 3550 switches were already running a modified version of the IOS, these devices are easily be integrated into this new paradigm. Minor changes in commands have been implemented on the 2950 and 3550 (which are not end-of-life, as are the others) to synchronize their command sets with the chassis-based switches running CatIOS. For example, the **port group** command on the 2950 and 3550 has been replaced with the **channel-group** command, and the **show port group** command on the 2950 and 3550 has been replaced with the **show etherchannel** command, consistent with the commands used on the Catalyst 4006 or 4500 with Supervisor Engine III or Supervisor IV Engine and Catalyst 6000 Family of switches running CatIOS.

Eventually, it is likely that the CatIOS will be called simply Cisco IOS. In other words, all Cisco routers and switches will run "Cisco IOS." This is evidenced partly by the fact that new releases of the Cisco IOS for the 2600, 3600, and 3700 series routers already support most of the switch commands available on the Catalyst 2950 and 3550 (although the routers require a 16- and 36-port Ethernet Switch Module to take advantage of these commands). It is also evidenced by the switch commands available on the Cisco 7600 series routers. However, in the transition phase that Cisco is now in, it can be argued that the term CatIOS serves as a preferable name to indicate what a speaker or writer is referring to when discussing modern Cisco platforms integrating switch and router functionality.

Notes

Notes